Author's Note

From the Top of the Dune

I stand at the top of a sand dune along the shore of Lake Michigan. Before me are twenty-two steps that lead down to the beach. The sun is setting, and the sky above reflects a purple afterglow. On the shore a fire has been set by scooping out a small depression and igniting kindling in the hole. The flame gets support from breezes wafting over it. This way, the fire burns slowly and thoroughly. Wood for the fire comes from the limbs of trees that have fallen from the face of the dune on to the beach. West winds work inexorably against the dune.

The glowing embers of the fire recall the beauty, the mystery, the joys and the sorrows that have filled my life.

Robert Cronin

The Glow of Embers

Fragments

with a twist !

Robert Cronin

Island Graphics
Printing & Design
459 Periwinkle Way
Sanibel Island, Florida 33957

Illustrations by Nancy Barnes

The author extends special recognition to
Nina Orrell
whose time, talent, and patience
made this book possible.

Robert J. Cronin
990 N. Lake Shore Dr., 5E
Chicago, Illinois 60611
(312) 943-3258

ISBN 0-9653081-0-3

To all the

Cranberry Bowlers,

especially the young Hot-Chocolateers.

Introduction

The Cranberry Bowl is a Thanksgiving morning touch football game followed by a light brunch. It is an extended family celebration, and has been around for a long time. Last Thanksgiving, eighty-some attended. Everybody is invited to play in the game—grandparents, moms and dads, uncles and aunts, nieces and nephews, friends, and most of all the children. Quite often, the ball carrier rides on the shoulders of an uncle. The game has been played in slush, in snow, in mud, or if we're lucky, on a dry field. Each year we joyfully welcome to the group the newest, littlest Hot-Chocolateer. This is a book of remembrances dedicated to all the children grown and small.

CONTENTS

I. Familia

II. The Dome for a Home

III. Along the Way

IV. A World Apart

V. Omega

Familia

MY MERRY OLDSMOBILE

Michael Cronin, my paternal grandpa, was rough and tough. He had a booming voice and a scowl. During the early 1900's, he traveled Wisconsin and upper Michigan for the Hines Lumber Company. He would buy stands of trees from the Indians who owned large tracts of forest. Dealing with Indians was like trading with Gypsies. The rules were constantly changing. Grandpa knew he was going to lose so he worked at keeping his losses as small as possible. The Indians celebrated when a deal was closed. Grandpa celebrated when he came to Chicago and the Hines people saw how much lumber they got for their money.

One summer morning in 1922, when I was seven years old, Grandpa banged open our front porch screen door and said in his loud voice, "We're going to the Dells!" The Dells is a resort area over a hundred miles north of Chicago.

Everyone started talking at once; I guess it was the Irish thing to do. Grandpa had bought a car—an Oldsmobile four-door touring car. It had a California top made of canvas, with isinglass windows which could be put up if it rained. My dad had to go and get the car from the dealer because Grandpa didn't drive, and didn't want to learn how. So one fine morning, when everyone was busy and no one had time for me, and the car was parked out front, we left for the Dells. The sun was shining.

My dad and my uncle Jim sat in the front where all the gears and things were. My mother and Grandpa sat in the back, and

Jim (my slightly older brother) and I sat between them on the floor. We couldn't see much, but it was our first trip and we were excited.

There were no highways then, just a map showing roads that would get us to the Dells. We had left home at 7 a.m., and should have gotten there by late afternoon. The sun kept shining and the morning was uneventful. We had two tires blow out on us, but that was to be expected. We stopped in a small town for lunch. When we came out, there were clouds and it looked like rain. Leaving town was no problem—there was only one road into the town and the same road out. About a half hour later, it began to drizzle.

We had just entered Wisconsin from our home state of Illinois. It didn't look different, though I thought it would. Then it began to rain, so we put up the canvas top with the isinglass windows. Soon it was raining harder. We came to a dip in the road, and stopped. A local farmer was standing there with a team of horses. The rain didn't seem to bother him or the horses. He was there to have his horses pull us through the water-filled section of road—for a price. Grandpa tried to haggle down the price. The farmer was slow to speak, and when he did, he told Grandpa that the price would be double if we tried to cross on our own and didn't make it. Grandpa was stubborn, so we tried it ourselves. Water clogged the exhaust pipe, and so the farmer took his time and we paid twice his fee. It was really raining now, and the California top wasn't equal to it. Grandpa told my uncle Jim, who was driving, to pull in at the next farm house, and we all got out and went inside. The farmer and his wife were friendly. People didn't drop in every day. Outside, thunder and lightning took charge. Kerosene lamps were lighted and tea was served—milk and cookies for my brother and me.

Suddenly the house was bright like a summer's day; outside you could see the road, the farmer's barn and silo, and even the corn fields. At the same time, the house gave a mighty thump and everything rattled. No one knew what to say. Mom got out her rosary. We couldn't figure out what was happening. After a while, the rain let up, and Grandpa was pushing us all to get going. Outside, the air smelled like it was burning. When we had driven a half mile or so, Grandpa told us the farmer and his wife worked with the devil. He even had a name for their religion, and we were lucky people to get out of there alive. Some years later, I found out that it was a meteor burning itself out in the farmer's corn field. Scientists say its diameter was about six feet. Today, only a very small part of it is above ground.

We continued to have tire problems. When we used the jack to raise the car, the base of the jack would go into the mud, and the car wouldn't rise. We got pieces of wood and branches from trees, and finally the comforter that Jim and I sat on was placed on the ground so the jack would raise the car. We had four extra tires tied to the back of the car, and several inner tubes under the front seat. We used them all. It was getting dark, and we seemed to be lost on a country road. When we came to a farmhouse that was all lit up, and had cows and horses and wagons outside, Grandpa said he would go and ask how far it was to Madison. We watched, and pretty soon there were people at the door and they were all laughing at Grandpa. He came back to the car and my mom kept telling him to be quiet—there were children in the car; I could hear what he was saying, but I didn't know any of the words. My grandfather was not a man of great patience. His vision of our trip to the Dells in the new Oldsmobile with the California top was quite different from the way it was turning out. He was wet and he was cold, and his new car was splattered all over with mud. It was dark, we were lost, and we were out of spare tires.

Well, we had no choice, so we plowed ahead and finally saw a sign saying that we were entering the great city of Madison, Wisconsin, close to the Dells. Our two back wheels had flat tires, and they made noise when we got to a brick road. There were a few people still outside, or on their front porches.

When we passed by, they would call out, "You've got a flat tire."

Grandpa, with his booming voice, would answer, "Go to hell!"

The day finally did end and we got out of our wet clothes and fell asleep.

At the Dells, there were boat rides, walking behind a water fall, climbing rocks to see the countryside, and stuff. I didn't mention it, but what I was really waiting for was the ride home. When the time came—with new tires, and inner tubes, and a sunny day—it was a flop. Nothing happened, we were home by three in the afternoon. I liked going there best.

KNICKERBOCKER CHRONICLE

His name was Bernard Kelly. He was my maternal grandfather. He was born in Ireland and later brought his wife, Anna Courtney, a son John, and two daughters, Kathryn and Emily, to Chicago. His first job was conductor on a cable car that ran from downtown to a nearby residential neighborhood taking people to and from work. It was in the early 1900s. The cable cars, front and back end, were open to the weather. The passengers sat inside by a stove. In front was the motorman who made the car move. In back was the conductor who collected fares.

A myth can be a story that comes down in a family from one generation to the next. It's told, not written. It's that family's story. So—

One very cold winter day with the wind howling and the conductor freezing, our Bernard Kelly made a decision. He went to the front of the car, gave his changer to the motorman and left the railroad forever. He had noticed on his many trips downtown that there was this large building kept warm in the winter and filled with laughing Irishmen—his own kind of people. Sure there were a few Poles and some Italians, but mostly they were Irish. This place was known by many Chicagoans as the steel works.

Now that's the problem. There was no steel made there. What they meant to say was *steal* works, and it was known to all as City Hall. So Bernard went in, met and mixed with his kin, and came out of the building in the springtime with a contract to do work for which he would get paid. He was now a business-man. The contract was to pave Michigan Avenue, even then Chicago's most prestigious street. What he didn't have was a company with horses and wagons and shovels, and all the things he would need to complete the work. People who made their living in politics didn't find it surprising that Bernard had a contract and no company. Nevertheless, he needed to find a company.

Well, there was a man in Chicago who had come from New York and he had a company. It turned out he didn't like it in the midwest with all these primitive people, and Indians as well. He wanted to go back east, and so Bernard bought his business. It wasn't much—a small office and yard, two wagons, and three horses. It was called Knickerbocker Paving Company (named after Father Knickerbocker, the founder of New York). It was not paving as we know it today. In those days, Knickerbocker's business was filling and leveling pot holes in the dirt or stone streets to make them smoother for the traffic.

Bernard Kelly took to business like a fish to water, and soon added roofing to the company name. Bernard became an entre-preneur. He opened a Knickerbocker operation in Minneapolis. He bought twelve prime blocks of real estate in the developing area of South Shore, a part of the growing Chicago. Bernard revived the paving part of Knickerbocker and laid streets and sidewalks in the developing community. Even today, the Knicker-bocker stamp can be seen embedded in the concrete to identify which company did the work. My brothers and I most remember the real estate.

Bernard disposed of the real estate too soon, as far as an investment went. He needed the money to help his wife and daughter. His wife had become ill so he sent her to Canada where the cool, clean air was purported to improve the health of people with TB, and he sent his older daughter to the hot, dry climate of Texas where she might recover from the devastating debilitation caused by a pneumonia siege. Neither remedy seemed to work.

Sadly, his wife, Anna, and daughter, Kathryn, died at early ages; Anna of TB, and Kathryn from the effects of pneumonia. Most people were said to have died of TB or pneumonia, since they didn't have names for all the different diseases as they do now.

Illness is expensive, so Bernard had to sell his real estate to pay the bills. His good friend who owned the adjoining property was able to keep his investment, and watch it grow into a multi-million dollar holding. This man's grandsons were peers of Bernard's grandsons, my brothers Jim, Mark, and myself. In their whole lives, I don't think those young men ever worked. They had cars, clothes, great homes, and they travelled the world. They were first class bums—and if Bernard had been able to hold on to his real estate, my brothers and I could have joined our peers in great debauchery—it's worth remembering.

My grandpa Bernard's only son, John, kept the breweries busy most of his life. In this regard, the Irish were well known as great consumers—they still are. So, the second daughter, Emily, buried her mother and her sister, and a year or so later, her father, Bernard Kelly. She also worked at making something, anything, of the brother, John. Her name was Emily Frances Kelly, and she was to be my mother.

Emily grew up, and taught children at a south side public school. It was at this time that she met my father, Mark Aloysius Cronin. Most young boys took the name Aloysius at their confirmation. Apparently young boys didn't make good saints, so we only had Aloysius to choose from. Those young men spent most of their lives trying to remember how to spell it.

Emily once told me that her courtship with Mark was not always peaches and cream. On Sunday, she would join her young man at Mass and be invited back to the Cronin's apartment for Sunday dinner. After the dinner dishes were cleaned, the three Cronin boys, Jim, Mark, and Raymond, along with their parents, Michael and Catherine, and a drop-in friend or so, would play poker all afternoon. Well, my mother didn't play poker, so she sat in the living room with the dog and pretended she cared about what she was reading. It was her feeling that Mark's mother looked less than kindly on her.

Emily was born in Ireland, and she had kept her age to herself. After Emily died, her granddaughter, Carol travelled to Ireland and discovered that Emily was four years older than Mark; so, it might have seemed that Emily was cradle-snatching Mrs. Catherine Cronin's handsome young son. Well, Mark and Emily did get married and they lived happily for many years.

Bernard Kelly died soon after Mark and Emily were married, and Emily became heir to Knickerbocker Roofing & Paving Company. When the will was probated, a kindly judge asked my father where he worked. He answered that he was a testing engineer for the Northwestern railroad. That meant he climbed outside the cab onto the boiler of the steam engine while it was moving to check on valve performance and things. The judge then asked him why he couldn't take a swing at learning and running the Knickerbocker business rather than having it put up for sale. What Mark learned in short order was that he, too, like Bernard, was a natural at running a small business.

With Mark Cronin at the head, Knickerbocker worked hard during the first year getting many contracts, doing a large volume of work, and making zilch. Mark's banker gave him some good advice. On every 10th job he bid, he should raise the price 25% to see what would happen. The next year, he tried it, and was overwhelmed to get the first job on which he boosted the price. From then on, all jobs carried the higher price and the Knickerbocker business prospered.

Knickerbocker became a favorite roofing contractor for some of the country's railroads. After World War I, travel was done for the most part by rail. It was the time of lavish meals and superb sleeping accommodations in what were known as *Pullman Cars*. The Illinois Central had buildings on their main line all the way to New Orleans. The Southern Pacific had Knickerbocker doing work all the way to Texas. It was easy for my dad to compete, as free freight for material and free travel for the workers was a part of the contract. Every fifty miles along a railroad right-of-way, there would be a large roundhouse, a sizable mechanical shop and other buildings. These facilities served the needs of passenger trains and monstrous freight train locomotives, both run by steam engines. The wooden roof decks and tar roofs on these facilities had to be replaced quite often, as the smoke and steam of the locomotives rotted the lumber and broke down the waterproofing tar products of the roof.

As a little boy during this time, I remember helping my dad to pack his bag. He told me that he was befriended by a railroad executive in charge of maintenance work. The executive discovered at a convention that my father didn't drink. The executive had a big thing against drinking and immediately took to my father as an abstinent friend. The executive had his own private car replete with all the amenities of the finest hotel; so the private car would be attached to a passenger train, or a freight train, whichever was headed in their direction, and the two of them would set off. During the night, or whenever the train came to a roundhouse installation, the private car would be shunted to a dead-end piece of track. In the morning, Dad and the executive would have breakfast (as I packed his bag, my dad would describe the strawberries and cream), and then Dad would go out and climb the various roofs in order to report what needed to be done. The executive, meanwhile, would seek out information about the nearest golf course, and the two of them would spend their afternoons playing golf. During the night, the private car would be coupled to a train, and for the rest of the work week it would go like that. Dad would come home with roofing contracts. He sure had charisma. I wonder who won at golf!

Mark and Emily, my parents, had five children—Jim, Bob, Dorothy, Kay, and Mark. The three boys eventually served apprenticeships as roofers to earn college educations, ending up at Knickerbocker where we took control of the operation when our father passed away.

During those years many advances took place in the industry. Machines replaced hard manual labor. New products and systems were tried out. Some old serious problems, however, remained. We lost five men during those years; three fell to their deaths and two were electrocuted by high voltage lines. Safety was emphasized, but familiarity sometimes breeds risk.

Steel mills and heavy industries replaced the railroad business that was so good to my father. Knickerbocker also entered the architectural sheet metal field, and that company became an integral part of the operation. Pension and profit-sharing plans made it possible for us to transfer our stock to our sons. The company continued with the policy that required stockholders to be working members of our small business. In that way, they would be participating and would know when business was good or bad. While I was president of the company, I don't think my brothers and I ever put any action to a vote. We talked things through until we could arrive at a mutual agreement. We have remained close friends all our lives, as well as ferocious golf competitors.

Our wives were a great source of comfort to us during those years. Family and business tended to overlap. Our wives allowed us to talk about our problems with them, but at no time did they ever interfere by bringing themselves into our business discussions. That was a great and important gift to the success of the company. We ran the business as a team for fifty years. The business continues to grow but it is now our time to step aside. The present generation at Knickerbocker is made up of some of our sons. The tradition carries on.

We worked hard, and were able to provide our wives with many of life's amenities, and our children with their college educations. God has been good to us. Now Knickerbocker's future is in the hands of our sons. May they do well.

In the distant wings, there are girls and boys schooling themselves to come center stage and in their time carry on the Knickerbocker tradition.

"BILLIE," MEMORIES OF MOM

Her name was Emily Frances Cronin (nee Kelly) and she was known as "Em" to her many friends, as "Billie" to the young swain who won her heart and as Mom to the five of us kids. The time was the early 1900s. In some ways she was ultraconservative and as far as politics or religion were concerned, neither was a fit subject for discussion at the dinner table. In case we lapsed, we were interrupted by Mom telling us what some woman she met on 71st Street (the local shopping area) said about the weather.

At the card table, Em was called the *sly fox*. She would smile quietly as she destroyed your holding. To shopkeepers she was a joy the moment she walked in, and the fountainhead of great sales. She was also a social bee flitting from luncheons to afternoon teas to catered dinner parties. She loved parties and gossiping. I remember one of her own dinner parties that had a rapid growth. It happened while she was making plans for the party. She called her husband, Mark—not for advice—just to prepare him. It seems she had a list of people she wanted to entertain, so she sat down by the phone to call them. Before she made her phone calls, however, she had prepared a substitute guest list in case any of the people on the first list were busy. She told her husband she hadn't made a mistake. It was just a slip-up between two sheets of paper. You guessed it—she invited all the substitutes to her party and they all could come!

"It could happen to anyone," she said, but what was she to do about her best friends who were going to be left out in the cold?

She called her caterer. Could he do the party for twice the number of guests? The answer was, "No way."

So she instructed the caterer to go ahead as planned for the original number of people. Undaunted, she called a second caterer to do a party on the same evening for the same number of guests. He could. My mother kept to the phone and invited all her friends from the first guest list; she just didn't mention to either of the caterers that they would be sharing the same kitchen, and left it to them to work out enough china, crystal, and everything else. The party was held, all the invited guests arrived, and everyone had a great time.

Afterwards, my father said, "There was more noise coming from the kitchen than from all the assembled guests in the living room!"

None of this bothered Em at all; she just waited for the dinner invitations from all her friends to start rolling in. When there were two parties on the same day and she couldn't attend both, it was a tough time for us kids—we took the brunt of her disappointment. As for me, I knew a dozen ways to disappear.

Negotiation was a skill in which my mother excelled. One evening, when the family business was going through hard times, my Dad sat down with Em, his Billie, at the dining room table to talk. He explained to her that the milkman who came down the alley with his horse and wagon each morning was raising the cost of his products. It had to do with unions or something. My dad didn't like it. So he explained to Em the family's need to economize—and he had a way she could help. Each day, the grocery store would call and Mom would place her order. Dad explained that milk was cheaper at the grocery store than when it was delivered by the milkman and since the groceries were delivered free, she could buy her milk there, rather than from her old friend Dan, the milkman, and his horse, Ronald. When Dad finished, Mom was quick to answer.

She said, "I'll never understand you, Mark, always complaining about how much I spend on this and that, and now you're telling me I should raise my grocery bill by adding milk!!" Well, Dad couldn't win them all. My mom and dad were such good friends they even had trouble arguing with each other.

When my sisters were in high school, the telephone bill skyrocketed. Dad thought outsiders were coming into his home just to use his phone. He was wrong there—my Mom and those sisters of mine were talking nonstop. Anyway, Dad acted, and our phone was replaced with a pay phone. It took a nickel in the slot to make a call. The next month, there was no phone bill—it was cash-and-carry and Dad was happy. The following month, when the telephone company came to collect their nickels from the box there was hell to pay! It seems Mom had learned at the hardware store that you could get fifty lead slugs for twenty-five cents, and each one would work the phone. The telephone company informed my dad that they just didn't fall for the plugged nickels, and he'd have to pay the difference. My mom had given it her best shot.

The episode I liked the best took place at our summer rental home where Dad taught us all to swim by age seven—although Mom didn't swim a stroke. All she would do is go out waist-deep, hold both of Dad's hands and bounce up and down. My dad didn't think much of this and he told her so. Seven-year-olds could swim, why couldn't she?

Then, one winter when it was snowy and plenty cold, my mother walked a block, got on a street car and took a ride. It was in the afternoon while we were at school. She went to the local YMCA where they had a pool. She sure knew how to keep a secret.

So, the next summer up in the country, she was out waist-deep in the water waiting for Dad. He came to her with the same old jargon.

She sort of egged him on, "Would it really mean that much to you if I could swim? How much?"

Dad finally mentioned a paltry amount.

She laughed, "Is that all it means to you?"

Meanwhile, she was backing away from him and asking again, "What about from here—and what about from here?"

Mom worked the reward for learning how to swim up to the price of a fur coat she had seen—she even mentioned the fur coat.

"Come here," Dad said, "Quit the fooling—if you could swim from over there to here, I'd buy the coat for you tomorrow." To his surprise Mom lowered herself into the water, pushed off and leisurely swam to him. (Her best friend who had recently bought a new fur coat was in for a surprise!)

Another incident I remember began one afternoon when a black man who had only one arm came to the front door. He wanted work and my mother felt sorry for him. My mother was always feeling sorry for people, so she told him to go to the back yard and start cleaning it up.

The next morning, my mother went to Mass—she liked to do that. (We would rather have had her around making breakfast, though.) On her way home, she saw a black man with one arm and she said to him, "Why aren't you working in my back yard?"

The man seemed confused. She even had to point out to him which house was hers.

Later that morning my sister asked, "What are you trying to do, Mom—collect one-armed black men out in the back yard?"

That was Em's way.

I remember years later when my dad died, his Billie—my mom—moved into the living room chair that was his. She hardly ever left it.

HELP!
MAIDS OF HONOR

Back in the 1920s, a few years after I was born, my mom said to my dad, "If I'm going to be your breeder, I'm going to need help."

Mom didn't mean anything personal, he didn't have to put on his pout face. She just needed *help*—like one or two little Irish girls right off the boat who she could train. She told him he shouldn't be so sensitive. He should just earn more money.

One time Mom told Dad that if they needed more money, he could stamp envelopes. She explained that she had read some-where about home industries as a way to riches. She just thought he wouldn't spend so much time talking about "finances," as he called it, if he could get rich doing some home industry after work and weekends. Mom was always trying to help others.

Well, pretty soon Mom hired Julia, the Polish strong-woman of *no nonsense*. Jim, my older brother, didn't like her. I didn't like her either, and when Dorothy arrived, we told her not to like Julia. Julia kept the house clean—and we were the problem makers. Julia didn't talk except to give orders, or blame us for messing up our rooms or such. I don't know what happened, if it was Mom or what, but during these years maids kept coming and going.

Next was Irma, and she talked about everything. She was short and kind of round, just nice; I could look at her all day while she talked. I didn't know why or what, it just made me feel nice. I was sorry when she left and I couldn't look at her any-more. Her leaving had to do with Thursday, maids' day off, when the maids got dressed up and went to the Trianon Ballroom to dance. (There were always more maids or maidens there than men.) I guess Irma didn't get home when she should have—what-ever—my mom had rules, and Irma went packing. I missed her.

Well, the next two you can have. They were fresh off the boat from Ireland—sassy as could be—always talking to each other, and laughing, and like my mom said, "hair-brains." They were young, they were here in the States, *so who's to care*. They were around for a year, a long enough time for Mom to give them her maids' education—you know—folding things, and polishing the silverware, and keeping the glasses shiny, and carpet sweeping, and such. When they left they made a dramatic exit. Work had been going on all day for a dinner party. The "Irishers" were to help the caterer or "cooking lady" in making the meal, then greet the guests on their arrival to help them to put their coats and hats away, and later serve the dinner. My brothers and sisters and I weren't really there on this occasion. We had been given our mom's strict rule, as well as our dad's, to stay upstairs in our rooms doing our homework and "no monkey-shines." That's when the "Miss Sassies" decided to quit. They packed their suitcases, and came down the front staircase. Mom and Dad were greeting the arriving guests and wondering why no one was there to take the guests' wraps. When, wouldn't you please, without a word to anyone, they pushed through the guests and out the front door. That was it, we never saw them again.

As Mom said, "And to think they are Irish." Mom's guests helped serve the dinner—that is, the women did.

Then one year at our summer house, we had a local maid working for us. She was young and pretty. Her name was Helen. One day when my mother was out playing cards, Helen baked some cookies and called me in to have some before any of the other kids. While we talked, she showed me that she had hurt her knee. It was red and bruised. She said she had fallen while walking back to the cottage on the evening of her day off. I didn't know why she had to walk home, since she had gone out with the milkman that evening. An innocent little boy was someone to share things with—probably because he never knew just what it was she was talking about. Friendships are nice when both parties get something out of the relationship. I got the cookies. Whenever I saw the milkman, however, I gave him my best scowl!

The next candidate to try my mother's patience was Marguerite Wilson, grey-haired, full of energy, and a superb cook. My erudite brother told us siblings that the word *marguerite*, was a synonym for *pearl*. He said we would save up on syllables if we just called her Pearl, and so that's what we did. What a smart brother! When Pearl's husband died, she left Tulsa, Oklahoma, where they lived, and came to Chicago to be with her daughter. How she came to work for us I don't know. She moved into the maid's room, and got to know us. We got to know Pearl. She was a real gem—full of fun, and the provider of great eats.

At this time, since Pearl was strictly a cook, Dosia would come up from the basement (where she lived) to do the housework. When Pearl left, she became her successor.

One snowy night, when my folks were going out, Pearl asked to see my mom. She offered Mom her mink coat to wear if Mom wanted it. Mom didn't own a mink, and this coat was a real quality product. Mom gave it the mirror treatment. She looked great—we told her so—but Mom said, "No." I guess she couldn't think of how to explain it to her friends. You can bet she got her own in a year or two, and my dad never even had to use any "home industry" to get rich.

During this time, my folks gave a dinner party for their friends, the Gorins. Jim Gorin's brother Frank and his wife were invited. They were on a visit from Oklahoma. So after cocktails, the guests all sat down at the dinner table. Shortly, the swinging door opened and in came Pearl with a leg of lamb. She was intent on putting it down when she heard the visitor from Oklahoma say, "My God, Frank, it's Marguerite Wilson."

The Gorins and the Wilsons socialized and mostly gambled on the horses together when Pearl was out in Tulsa. Pearl greeted them by their first names, then she retired to the kitchen and stayed there. My older brother, Jim, was called down to serve the rest of the meal. I guess Pearl's husband loved to gamble, was down on his luck at the time of his sickness, and Pearl was left with little. So she came to Chicago to be near her daughter.

Pearl had led the good life and liked it. On her Thursdays off, she would spend her time at Con Cokley's neighborhood bar, sitting close to the resident bookie. People liked her, so she socialized—drinking and betting, and having one more until way past closing hour. Con Cokley was a talker you couldn't shut up. Well, one Friday morning, Mom cooked our breakfast (good but no frills), and we ignored the fact that Pearl was still sleeping—she must have really gotten in late on her Thursday off. Coincidentally, on that particular Friday, we were all out during the day—Dad at his office, Mother at Marshall Field's for lunch and shopping, and us kids slaving away at school. Since it was winter, daylight ended about dinner time. When we sat down at the dinner table, we heard some humming in the kitchen and waited to be served. Pearl came through the swinging door laden with oatmeal, bacon and eggs. Then in a minute, she returned with my dad's hot coffee. She held the cup in one hand and the saucer in the other, rattling the two against each other, and stabilizing herself for a safe landing. There was enough light outside to give the appearance of your usual gray dawn. Mom gave us her *no giggling* look, and we all ate our breakfast again—two in one day. Pearl's was better!

During her kitchen reign, Pearl provoked her employer, my mom, on several other occasions. I remember the day when Mom definitely fired Pearl. I don't know what Pearl's indiscretion was, but it probably had to do with socializing at Con Cokley's. Well, Pearl came down the front stairs with her packed bag, and Mom stood at the foot of the stairs with severance money. Pearl put down her bag to say goodbye. Under her arm she carried what looked like an afghan. Mom gave Pearl the money due her. Then Pearl presented Mom with the afghan, which was very beautiful and had a large green "C" crocheted in the middle. She said that she'd just finished it the night before, that it was made especially for Mom, and Pearl wanted her to have it. By the time Pearl got to our front steps Mom was crying, and Pearl had pulled it off once again. She asked me to help carry the bag back upstairs. We had a great dinner that night!

Some time later, on a summer night, we heard the front doorbell ringing at a very late hour. Dad went to the door concerned about who could possibly be there. It was a cabby who asked him if he was Mr. Cronin.

He answered, "Yes," and the cabby said, "I got your old lady, Mrs. Cronin, out in the cab. She's soused. Help me carry her in."

My mother was in the parlor and heard the conversation. Well, my dad and the cabby got Pearl out of the cab—she didn't weigh that much—into the house, and up to her room. As he came upstairs, Dad said in a loud voice, "Close your doors and stay in your rooms."

By his very tone, we knew we'd best obey. When Father paid the cabby, he asked how he had gotten the name, Cronin, for his fare. The cabby said that he worked Con Cokley's all the time, and that everyone there called her "Mrs. Cronin."

My mother went up and put Pearl to bed. She was awake late that night as she struggled with her pride. She also realized how much she loved this little lady who was always gay, always upbeat, a friend to all of us, and a great cook for the family and for parties. Pearl would be hard to replace. As usual, Pearl won out—she stayed. My father got to know the cabby, who then became responsible for bringing Pearl home and monitoring her imbibing. The cabby was also directed to straighten up the identification bit; it was my mother who gave him those instructions. Pearl stayed on—a joy to us all. In time, Pearl's daughter called and said her mother didn't have to work anymore. We all kissed Pearl goodbye.

Our next cook was Dosia Montgomery. She came to our house when I was seven. She seemed to me to be large and black. She wasn't large, I was small. On Mondays she would come in from the alley, go into the basement, turn on the gas under the large kettle of water and start the day's washing. Sometime during the morning, you could hear her whacking the clothes with a large wooden paddle.

Our basement was dark, with bare walls, a furnace, a room to store coal, and a place to pile ashes; but the basement had another room, which the carpenter had paneled, and that's where the billiard table was. My dad played billiards and taught it to his sons, whether we wanted to learn or not. When we sulked, he had our sisters give it a try. Thank goodness our mom declared billiards to be unladylike before the girls could beat us.

On Tuesdays, clothes poles were set up in the backyard. The sheets and clothes and all would blow so pretty in the breeze, and then there would be the smell of things ironed—done with a hot piece of metal attached to a wooden handle. Tuesday nights Dosia went home. Every week that's the way it was.

During these years, taking ashes from the basement, up the stairs, through the yard, and out to the alley was a pain in the behind. It seemed to go on forever, until one day we came home from school, and there was a big hole in the yard where Dosia always dried our clothes. Next day, they put an oil tank in the hole and covered it up. No more ashes, no more banking the furnace at night and hoping there would be a fire in the morning. Now it was oil, and nobody had to do anything. That's when my mother and Dosia had a talk. The carpenter was called to fix up the former coal room, and Dosia came to live with us. Besides doing the wash, she would keep house while Pearl did the cooking. She thanked my mom for taking her in.

Dosia Montgomery was happy in our home. She was a Baptist, active in her church. Then, after some studying, she decided to baptize into the Catholic faith—the only black member of our parish. She became, like Pearl, a part of the family—though not in name—in fact. Taking center stage as Pearl's successor was an unlikely role for Dosia, yet she took over Pearl's job of cooking and did whatever else she could. As Dosia grew old, we grew up. In time, our mother assigned us to the chores that Dosia could no longer handle. When she died, we were all in attendance at her funeral.

Times were changing, our household was changing, and we all learned how to do for ourselves.

The Glow of Embers

MY DAD

My dad had a smile that would break your heart—break it open to love. I mean he gave you his attention in a way that seemed to be giving you himself. It was wonderfully warm to be near him. He enjoyed life and enjoyed sharing his life with others. The way I remember it, the front door of our house seemed to be nailed open. Everyone was welcome. My dad was a successful businessman and the head of our family. As for his roofing business, people preferred to trust *his word* rather than climb up a ladder to see whether their own roof needed replacement.

Many of Dad's friends were doctors, and they often told him that he should join their ranks. Patients need caring, and assurance, and that's what my dad had to give—to his wife, to his five children, and especially to those he met during his lifetime who were less fortunate than he was.

We all have faults and I'm sure Dad was no different, but I never found out what they were and I don't recall my mother pointing them out to me.

Growing up in our home was a gentle and kind experience for my sisters, my brothers, and myself. I remember back during the 1929 depression, hearing my mother insist that my father go with her to a neighborhood movie-house a few blocks from our home. She said she needed the plate, or glass, or piece of silverware that was given to anyone buying a ticket. One morning during those times, I heard my mom suggesting the same idea to a friend. Mom was recommending that her friend take the "bread winner" (who wasn't sure where his next penny was coming from) to a movie so he wouldn't drive himself mad with worry. It wasn't about the plate, and it wasn't about the show, it was the best thing she could think of doing for the man she loved who felt the weight of the world on his shoulders each morning when he awoke. The movie might allow him a few moments of distraction, particularly if it was a western with lots of action. It may have helped, because we lived through the hard times until the day when both my parents could smile again.

I remember a Good Friday when my father ended the day smiling—it didn't come easily. It happened in 1936, at a time when all the Catholics were pious; from noon until three o'clock the churches would have standing room only. So it would be no surprise that my father was in a church downtown on that Good Friday. But praying—he wasn't, for all his efforts to pray got nowhere. Business, another center on which his life revolved, was winning over his mind and heart and making inroads on his soul.

"Damn it," he said quietly to himself. It didn't help. By now he was sweating even though the church was cool enough for coats. It was the devil hunkering around (he always gives off a lot of heat).

Dad's quandary had to do with a roofing contract he had been trying to win. He knew the corporate people were to decide who would get it that day. They had said so. Dad kept trying to pray, but there was this contract, and it might be let this day. He'd worked hard, and if only he could be there, he might be able to do something to secure the contract. Had the devil gotten into the church and chosen my dad as his target? Dad was sweating even more now.

So he made up his mind to leave—how it happened, he never knew—all the while realizing he could be done in at any moment by the demons. If he were German, Italian, Eskimo, or anything else but Irish, it would not be like this.

Well, he wasn't struck down, so he went to the office of the corporation where the contract was to be let. He was welcomed with open arms. They wanted to settle things and they needed information. He obliged, and a contract was drawn up, signed, and dated. Next to the date, they also put down the time—it was 3 p.m. Christ was dead, the ordeal was over, and my dad could relax.

By that evening, Dad had worked it around so that it was God that drove him out of the church—so he could get the contract. Amen!

Looking back, I realize that there were a lot of people like my dad and mom. Generous and kind, and motivating their kids to do better because they knew they could. There was discipline; there were all sorts of rules to be obeyed, and there were standards of conduct required. Cleanliness was a must. Clothing was to be hung up and kept neat. If you got in trouble at school, it didn't help you to try to put the blame on the teacher or anyone else because that wouldn't get you off the hook. When trouble came—and trouble was a part of everybody's experience—it was struggled with. There was no walking away, no carping, you just faced up to it. I remember the city officials coming to our house, taking down a quarantine sign for scarlet fever, and then putting one up for diphtheria. My mom had just finished six weeks of confinement with my brother, Mark, and was then given another six weeks at home with my sister, Kay. No leaving the house for anything, and no one was allowed in. Groceries were left on the door step. The rest of us kids went to stay with relatives, and my dad took a room in a hotel. There was more to come—we still had whooping cough and measles ahead of us. That was before the era of immunization shots, which changed all that.

I try to be like my dad. It takes patience, and holding one's tongue. It takes time spent with the family, and a fair amount of disappointment. But what I've learned is the joy I'm having in being, for a short while, so important and so loved in return by my children; and for me it's all been extended. There is a role for me now that in some ways is different, and in some ways the same—I'm a grandparent. It's greatly rewarding, and less demanding or responsible. The young ones and I enter the delightful world of imagination. We're all on our make-believe horses, and each horse has a name. We ride through the woods and all sorts of things happen. When we come home, Grandpa can get away with serving all those limited or forbidden foods— junk food and plenty of bacon. What a ball! And when the little ones get tired and cranky, it's their parents who show up for the job that requires patience—and Grandpa can fall into his easy chair for a quiet nap.

I am glad I had my dad for a teacher. I didn't know then how much fun he had with me—one of his children. I do now.

ERIN GO BRAGH

It was March 17, 1937, a warm, sunny St. Patrick's Day. Pat Kelly and Mike McShane, strapping fellows and good friends, were taking a stroll over to the shopping area by the el tracks on 63rd Street. They were interested in eyeing the passing lassies, and checking out their own handsomely reflected images in the shop windows. Of a moment, they both recognized a lad coming down the street, and greeted him.

Pat said "Hi, Bob."

Mike said "Hi, Jim."

The Irisher looked at each of them, said "The top of the marnin' to ya," and went on.

So, it all began quite casually; Pat and Mike talking at once, each correcting the other, each trying to explain the right name of this friend.

"Well," said Pat, "what's his last name?"

"It's Cronin," said Mike.

"Wouldn't you know—at least we're talking about the same guy—you've just got the first name wrong."

"Now wait a minute," said Mike. "Bob and I work on the street repair crew together. I'm with him every day."

Pat couldn't wait for him to finish. "You're crazy as a loon. Back home in Iowa, a couple of years ago, this lad came visiting his grandparents. He was from Chicago. We played 'Kick the Can' together on many afternoons along the town's dusty roads.

His name is Jim Cronin. Don't tell me I don't know him—that's Jim Cronin!"

It kept on like this until their noses were getting closer and closer. If it weren't such a lovely morning, they might have started a brawl, as good Hibernians are apt to do. Instead, they decided to walk over to the Cronin residence which they knew to be a few short blocks away. As they walked, they placed a wager. The loser would pay for lunch.

On 62nd Place, the Cronin's brick residence had a wide front porch, and sitting there with his shoes off, reading the *Chicago Tribune*, was Mark Cronin, the father. Mark, struggling through the Great Depression of the 1930s, was accustomed to using every resource he had at his disposal to keep bread and gravy on the table, along with an occasional piece of lamb for a stew. A wife and five children had to be fed. His two oldest, Jim and Bob, were of an age to work, if work could be found. So, whenever Mark went to church socials or such, he would mention his two sons, whom he would describe as "such fine specimens of manhood" who would work for "whatever—even a dollar a day." Both Jim and Bob had been graduated from high school, and hoped to get jobs. Some day they might even be able to start earning their way through college.

Mark was persistent, he kept asking, and then one day he hit pay dirt. It was just before the Christmas holidays of 1936, and the Cronin family received the best possible present. Alderman Flanagan gave Mark a call to say that he had found a spot with a street repair crew where he could put one of the boys to work, and he asked for the kid's name.

Well, Mark had a couple of good prospects he was working on for Jim, so he gave Bob's name.

The politician said, "Fine, you say his name is Bob—he starts Monday."

Sometimes lightning does strike twice. It happened at the Drexel Bank the next day. While Mark was taking care of some business, the bank president called him over and said how much he liked Mark's son, Bob. If Bob could be at the bank Monday morning, the banker would hire him as a runner. It seems Bob was frequently over at the bank president's house, courting one of the banker's daughters. Now Bob had two jobs, while Jim had none.

You'd think there was no problem—you just call the alderman, and say that come Monday, you will be sending son Jim to work with the repair crew instead of Bob. Well, there's just no way that could be done. Mark knew that by now Bob's name had been listed for the job, and if Mark called Alderman Flanagan— the one of the "short wick"—asking for any change, it would end up killing the deal. The alderman didn't like being told anything by anybody. On the other hand, with Bob knowing the bank president's daughter, it could be that something was afoot there. If Mark were to tell the president of the bank he would be sending a replacement, it might not set well.

So, Mark sat down with his two sons telling them what a help they would be to him by contributing to the family income. Jobs were scarce, money was difficult to come by, and eventually when he felt they understood these concerns, he began to explain what he had in mind. It could be called an "unintentional deception." It would only be until he could find a way to work it out. What he wanted was for both of his sons to be Bob Cronin. The burden was laid on Jim who would be working on the street crew. Could Jim handle being Bob for awhile, at least at work? Jim wasn't sure he wanted to be a part of this "unintentional deception," but if his dad wanted him to do it, he'd give it a try. Mark thanked his sons for their cooperation. Both boys started work on Monday morning, and soon Mrs. Cronin's larder was replete with meat, vegetables, and groceries of every sort.

So it was about 11:00 a.m. on this St. Patrick's morning of 1936 that Pat Kelly and Mike McShane walked up to the front porch of the Cronin residence and knocked on the wooden frame of the screen door. Mark Cronin put on his shoes and hooked, laced, and tied them. He looked for a coat that wasn't there, and walked over to open the screen door, all the while giving the lads a hearty welcome.

The young men sat down, and soon told Mr. Cronin of their wager. Could he tell them, please, the name of his son. Well, first Mark Cronin needed time to think. He was going to ask Pat and Mike to join him in a bit of St. Patrick libation. Then he remembered, as a true Irishman, he would never be the one to give a lad or lassie their first nip. This would be a dry sit-down.

So, Mark began by saying, "Well, I'll tell you, I just don't know who you saw this morning. These kids of mine come and go. It could even have been one of their cousins. You know how it is with us Catholics. Sometimes at dinner, I ask if we're feeding a neighbor or two along with our own. They all look alike."

From this he went on to the Depression, the Poles getting into politics, a couple of whacks at the English—all standard stuff. He then moved on to St. Patrick's Day and how that great man drove the snakes out of Ireland—though some say the snakes just gave up on the place—and how St. Patrick would have bashed that apple-touting serpent if he'd been in the Garden of Eden. Soon the confused lads were on their feet, and clearly anxious to leave. Mark apologized for not being able to help them and sent them on their way.

Pat and Mike left the porch and were halfway down the pike, before they began to wonder who was *who*, and what was *what*. It seemed they were going to spend the rest of their day with this conundrum. When they came to a street corner, there were two lassies among the noon strollers, and nice-looking ones, too. As the lads approached, a lace hanky slipped or fell free and fluttered to the pavement. A stalwart Mike was quick to the rescue, and the "little love messenger" was returned to its owner. Well, first things first. To hell with the Cronins—they would deal with that later. For the lads, this was the beginning of one grand St. Patrick's celebration.

Back on the Cronin's porch, Mark untied and unhooked his shoelaces. His libation was down to the last dram. He was thinking about truth and deception. Should he fault himself for being oblique? Life was uncertain in so many ways, and being Irish was simply a complex experience. Maybe he'd best go over to church, step into the box and confess this "unintentional deception" thing to Father Kevin and let him worry it through. He'd do that.

It was after Pat Kelly and Mike McShane had enjoyed the St. Patrick's Day festivities that they once again reflected on the Bob-Jim confusion. They would see what they could do about it. It didn't take long. A few questions here and a comment or so there. The Irish are great talkers, and out of it came the truth. The street worker was Jim Cronin pretending to be his brother Bob.

By evening, the rumored truth got back to Alderman Flanagan of the "short wick." Early next morning, he told the foreman of the street crew he wanted Bob Cronin sent to his office. When "Bob" arrived, the alderman told him to sit down.

Alderman Flanagan then rose from his chair, stood in front of the lad and said, "I want the truth, no blarney, you tell me what's going on."

Jim put his head down, and said nothing.

The alderman waited, and then said "Well, I'll call your father and maybe he can tell me why you're playing games with me."

So "Bob," who was really Jim, thought of his dad, and his good but mistaken "unintentional deception" thing. He started to talk slowly, and then with intensity, about his father and how it all happened. The short-wicked politician listened. When it was all told, and the alderman understood what had gone on, he gave out a grunt that might even have been a laugh.

"Go back to work, lad, and use your own name. If it'll make you and your father feel any better, you can tell him. So much for deception. Wasn't our own great St. Patrick himself a Frenchman?!?"

THE ART OF PLUMBING

My uncle Jim was six feet, two inches tall. During World War I, he made a friend in the service named Eugene Kirsting. They were both in the Navy assigned to a vessel resting on the sand of Lake Michigan by the side of a pier in Chicago. It was a large vessel, and the Navy's headquarters for the area. Keeping watch was of minimal importance on the ship, as there was never much danger of it being bombarded by one of the Kaiser's warships. As for U-Boat torpedoes, what was there to sink?

Today, seventy years later, a couple of miles away at the Museum of Science and Industry, there is a German U-Boat on the lawn next to the building. It's been there a long time. Some old people will tell you it was trucked in from the east coast by the "Heinies" (that's what Germans were called during WWI) to sink the sunken ship, our Navy headquarters. It's true—you can come to Chicago and climb into that sub; don't worry, it can't sink.

During the war, Uncle Jim and his new friend, Eugene, did plumbing work around the city at the homes of Navy personnel, including the suburban estate of the resident admiral. He was one of the first Navy officers to be given the title of "rear;" he was a rear admiral, and he was certainly qualified to be one. Just about the time that the Navy was running out of plumbing assignments, the war ended. My uncle and Eugene each got a medal and discharge papers. The day they left, they put on their Navy uniforms. They looked mighty good in them. The uniforms had only been worn twice before, both times for Fourth of July parades.

They walked home from the war since they both lived on Chicago's South Side. They put their uniforms in mothballs, and spent the rest of their lives together. Later on, when it was almost too late, they found mates and took time off to get married. It was no intrusion on their friendship.

I came to know them when they rented a space large enough for a desk, two chairs, and a phone in my dad's office. They were in the plumbing business. They did neighborhood plumbing repairs. Actually, it was a sideline to their "specialty" business. Uncle Jim's specialty was collecting a certain kind of cast iron metal container called a match-face. That's where people kept their lucifers. You know, you can still see them in farmhouse kitchens. The match-face was a small container hung on the kitchen wall and was the repository for lucifers, which were matches made of splinters of wood with man-sized sulphur heads. Scratch a lucifer against anything abrasive or, if you were an expert, the seat of your pants or thereabouts, and you could ignite a respectable flame. You could light a gas range (all four burners), the stove or oven, the hot water heater, and your cigar—all on one match.

If you've spent a lifetime trying to get a flame from one of those cardboard folded paper match containers—with a flap to be opened and closed before you can go to work on the match—you've really been deprived! If you're working and your clothes are sweaty, you're done for—right? No light! Or have you ever tried to light a candle when the wick has been mushed down in the tallow? Well, if you have, I'll tell you what you'll get with your paper matches. You'll get a tiny flame on a little piece of cardboard that is three-quarters of an inch from your fingers with no strength to dig out the wick, and a good chance of smelling burning flesh—yours. Or when the dregs of a tobacco pouch are dumped into the bottom of a pipe bowl—who's to go down to give it a light? Not your cardboard pipsqueak! It takes a lucifer with a real sulphur flame at the end of a wooden splinter to do the job. Just watch the sheriff in an old movie when he stands outside the door of his office to survey Main Street. He'll light up a lucifer with the seat of his pants and take the flame to the bottom of the bowl calmly.

So my uncle Jim collected cast iron lucifer containers that hung on the walls of people's kitchens. They came in all sorts of beautiful designs—a proper receptacle for lucifers—the real man's match. (I liked the designs with the lucifers stored in an icon's open mouth.) If you don't see home plumbing as a noble profession, you can still admire this artistic byproduct. Here I am going on about Uncle Jim and his specialty, forgetting his friend, Eugene, who was an equally avid collector. His field was fine glassware—goblets and such that gave off a heavenly tinkle when the rim of a glass was flicked.

So here's what those two giants did when they got a plumbing service call to go to a customer's home to fix a plugged toilet or whatever. (It was an age of innocence—can you imagine inviting those giants into your home today?) First they'd look in the basement, and then they'd go up into the attic. If the customer stored forgotten junk somewhere else, like out in a shed or garage, they'd search there too. Sometimes owners would get curious and ask questions. They would be right there with an explanation. They'd use scientific language and plumbing jargon—all about elbows and nipples, and female fittings—and that would send the owner packing, at least if it was the wife.

Don't be mistaken, they were honest men. Whatever they found that had to do with their specialty collections, they'd show the homeowner. Then they would haggle away, reducing their plumbing charges in exchange for the loot. Did I mention that both of their wives worked? That must have been a great help in covering living expenses for their families.

As far as talk goes, those two plumbers could out-talk any ordinary long-winded Irishman. They would come back to their

little office space after calling on a customer, set out their arti-
facts on the desk, and admire away. Everyone in the office
worked hard to avoid being brought into the discussion. If no one
was around, they'd just chatter on between themselves.

So it went day after day. They would sit there waiting for the
phone to ring, hoping for a new challenge, all the time talking up
a surpluscitity. When there were misunderstandings, such as
when one or the other forgot to bring a tool they needed, they
didn't let it grow into an argument. They just kept going over the
matter from every angle, again and again, until they got bored.
Then they'd notice something about the people on the street—
what they wore or didn't wear, or anything at all, and be off on
a new tack. Maybe they didn't get to talk at home! I never
thought of that. If the wives had worked all day, I doubt they
could go at the chatter with the intensity their husbands were
wont to. I know that on Saturdays, their wives were always gone
from the house to beauty parlors or shopping.

Everything the plumbers did took twice the ordinary time
required, because each step had to be talked about and evaluated
before they moved to the next step. Also, as they got old, uncle
Jim used to get angry. He would get angry at whatever they'd be
repairing. He mostly took his anger out on broken toilets, and
even sometimes on the toilet's owner. Eugene would be the
diplomat, getting Jim to lower his voice, or talking louder than
Jim so the customer wouldn't be aware of my uncle's profanity.
It finally got to the point where Uncle Jim couldn't face another
toilet, and would go out and sit in the truck and sulk until Eugene
finished the job and joined him. When their phone did ring, they
would ask my dad's secretary or me to answer it and take the
message. It used to bother me. If it was a repeat call, and they
had already ransacked the residence, they wouldn't return the
call. When I questioned them about this, they explained to me
that it had to do with their extreme dedication to their search for
art. It would be a real waste of time to go over to a house they
had already picked clean. This went on for some years before

their phone stopped ringing altogether. They were retired from business by a dead phone. Their wives, however, decided to keep working.

Since they no longer rented space in the office, they were soon out of sight and out of mind, until one day when they stopped by to talk to my dad. They were now traveling salesmen. They loaded their wares from years of collecting, and traveled from flea market to flea market around the mid west. They were amazed at the money they were making. They would sell and buy lucifer match containers and fine glassware. They didn't look too prosperous to me, and their wives stayed on at their jobs.

Gradually they grew old. It didn't diminish their friendship; they felt lucky to have each other. From the time they met, they did indeed live their lives together; and when they died, it was within a week of one another.

The Dome for a Home

The Glow of Embers

40

PREP'ING FOR NOTRE DAME
1929–1933

It took three street cars, with waiting in between, to get to St. Leo High School, and three more to get home. Rain, wind, and snow sure made it messy. Not only that, it wasn't easy getting to go to that school in the first place.

In grammar school I won a silver medal. Nothing had happened to me 'til then, and what happened afterwards wasn't good. Until the medal thing came along, I felt very comfortable. You see I was lucky to have an older brother to please my parents. He was an asthmatic, aesthetic, brilliant student who won gold medals. So I said to myself, if I could win a medal, my mom would stop looking at me with that worried expression. My competition for the silver medal was named Jane. She was much taller than I and she lived closer to church. Each morning in the classroom, Jane and I would paste up another silver star showing we had been to Mass that morning. The rest of our classmates had slept-out weeks ago. It was a two-horse race and I won. Jane got pneumonia (later she got well). My mom smiled at me and I thought her worries were over, but it got worse instead of better for me. The nuns had decided I was priest material and told my mom. So my mom started treating me like I was her only child and she quit worrying. I didn't. When the recruiter from the local Catholic high school for boys, a short streetcar ride away, came to visit our grammar school, I wasn't around. The nun-principal had called me and a couple of other nerds into her office and told us that because we were such fine boys we could have the afternoon off and go home. She gave us chocolate soda money as a present. It seems we were not to be contaminated by the recruiter.

Wouldn't you know, a couple of weeks later the Pope expressed his preference that high school classes become co-ed. Now the order of nuns at our grammar school also had a girls' high school one block from my home, called Aquinas. The nuns, obedient to the Pope's pleasure, announced that the following year their school would become co-ed. They even hired a well-known high school person to teach, coach, and recruit young men to enroll at Aquinas. That was good thinking! The Pope never knew he created a problem for the grammar school nuns—should they push for me to go to the seminary or Aquinas? Even so, I never seriously considered Aquinas because I could hardly live in the same world with girls, much less go to high school with them. And that includes my sisters. They were scary. If they looked at me I blushed! It's hard to explain.

So I turned up at St. Leo High School where my older brother went—three lousy streetcar rides away—and spent four of the happiest years of my life. At Leo, I pursued with life-threatening intensity (I did, you'll see) a career in basketball. As a freshman I was a flyweight at 113 pounds, sophomore year a bantamweight at one 123 pounds, junior year a lightweight at 135 pounds, and senior year a heavyweight. I stayed after school every day and practiced, until I had to take those freezing trollies home for supper. I would arrive still sweaty, and there would be my sisters who saw men, mostly me, as the most curious of creatures.

They watched me like a hawk. "Mom, why doesn't he take off his hat?" (Felt hats called crushers were permanently attached to the heads of all Leo students.) "Why doesn't he take a bath?" "Why is his face all broken out?" I got no peace.

It was the weight restrictions that brought on the trouble—deep trouble. It was during my junior year when the basketball season was about over. During the last year I had shot up like a reed to six foot one—a real thin reed. I got the flu and our family doctor came to our house to make a sick visit. Hard to believe, but that's what doctors did each morning. They rode around and visited their sick patients at home. Our doctor carried a little black bag, and there was a hammer in it to bang your knee, and some wired thing to talk to your heart, and some little flat sticks that pushed down your tongue until you felt like you might up-chuck, plus a searchlight to look in your ear and make you blind in the eye. He also had lots of little jars filled with pills.

When the doctor saw me he seemed startled. He first assured himself that my vital organs were in order and then left the room to visit with my mom. The doctor told her he thought I might have tuberculosis. How could I spring up to six feet and be losing weight rather than gaining? My mother thought my weight prob-lem could have something to do with basketball, my true love. She said she tried to encourage me to eat, but all I would do was just drink tea (gallons of it), with some toast. The medical man returned to my bedroom on the third floor. I thought climbing the stair had caused his reddened face. I was wrong.

He asked, "What does this tea business have to do with basketball?" I told him that teams were restricted by weight, and you had to get on a scale before each game to qualify.

He was one angry doctor. He ordered me to stay home for a week and just eat—or I could die! Well, it was still a choice! I gave in though, and the food was good. I ate like a horse and gained five and a half pounds by the time the Doc made his next visit. Anyway, I would play on the "heavies" the next year, and there would be no limit on weight. Besides basketball, nothing much happened in high school. You know, you do what you have to do to get by.

my senior year our basketball team won the —a first for the new school. The Senior Prom ll the team players were to get dates and go. called up my girl friend Margery. When I grammar school, they had a dinner in the the boys was assigned a girl to bring. We were to go to their homes, walk them to school, and walk them back home afterwards. We also were to sit with them during the dinner. Margery had moved, but not too far, so I called and she remembered me. We had a second date. We weren't going steady. That idea wasn't so smart because my dad wanted me to go to the University of Notre Dame, and they might have a dance and it would be easier for me if she was my steady. My sisters had a lot to say about my social life—none of it good. My mom, too, the one who was into the priest thing, was full of caution.

When it came time to be graduated from St. Leo, things got serious. Very few students could afford or even wanted to go on to college. You would lose four years of seniority in the work place when you finally took a job. If your dad worked for Hunding Dairy, he could get you a horse, a wagon, and a route, and you'd be set for life. For me it had been settled. My father was a Notre Dame nut and it had been decided years before that his sons would go there to college. Dad had been going to the football games of that great school for many years. You see, men like my dad were known as the *synthetic alumni*, or *sidewalk alumni*. They hadn't gone to Notre Dame, they just adopted it as their school. Well, my dad was Irish and sometimes he'd exaggerate things just a little. He told Mom and his friends that sending those boys to Notre Dame would set him back a fortune.

"Actually," he said, "counting everything, it would run a thousand dollars a year for each son." It was really more like nine hundred and ten the way I saw it, if he didn't throw in our clothes, our dentist bills, and our shots—stuff like that.

What he got for his money was the best farm-grown food in the world, and as much as we could eat; maid service by women who would come into our rooms, make our beds, vacuum the floor and empty the wastebaskets—every day! There was also an infirmary and medical care, with warm and loving nun-nurses who treated us just like our mom would when we were sick; plus books which didn't cost much anyway; a swimming pool, a girl's school next door; and most of all, a good football team. That's what my dad's money got—and an education.

The summer before I left for this institution of higher learning, I went to work emptying the oil from automobiles and putting in fresh oil for a dollar a day and lunch. The owner had a filling station and a bar where he provided free lunch for beer-drinking workmen. When fall came, I left for college with dirty fingernails and oil-stained hands. Even my mom couldn't get them clean.

It would be my first time away from home. My mom loaded me with food and nonstop instructions, and my dad purchased season tickets for the football games. I was glad because leaving home can be a lonesome experience. I didn't yet know about the fun I'd have and the characters I'd meet. I loved it!

The Glow of Embers

THE PASSING OF DICK'S WATER
1934

Dick's dad waited until the very last minute to say yes. My dad met him on the street in our neighborhood, and sweet-talked him into it. So it was settled: Dick and I would both be going to Notre Dame as freshmen. This pleased me because Dick was a confident young fellow, a year older than I was, and sure of himself. He could do lots of things. He could make fun of people—the other guys—and they didn't mind, they kind of liked it.

If I tried to joke like that, it was, "What do you mean?" and trouble. We liked each other and that was good, but we were different.

I remember a few years before when my dad, for what reason I'll never know, gave my brother and me boxing gloves for Christmas. As I look back now, I realize they were small pillows. It still didn't make sense, since he was spending a fortune to straighten out our teeth. We both went to this orthodontist, who would talk to his nurse while he worked which would provide me with some outstanding "bad thoughts" to remember for my next confession.

My brother Jim had asthma. During the night he would wheeze away, and I would be praying that it wouldn't stop, because if it stopped he would be dead—I thought. Jim and I tried on the boxing gloves once at Dad's suggestion or, rather, at his direction. Jim was two years older—we were probably 14 and 12.

My dad gave us instructions on how to stand, where to hold our hands, everything except how to keep from crying if we got hit too hard. Crying had recently become unmanly; I don't know who said so, the priests, or the nuns, or my mom, or maybe it was just the other guys I hung around with. Well, we went out in the backyard and fought three rounds. It amounted to zilch. We both sparred, which meant you made a move like you were going to light into the other guy, but you didn't. Neither of us got hurt, and I think my dad gave up hope of having a boxing champ in the family. Boxing was left to Jack Dempsey, Luis Firpo, Gene Tunney, and others. Since I remember their names, boxing must have been important at the time. At least it was to my dad.

A few years later in that same backyard, I boxed again, only this time it was with my roommate-to-be, Dick. I took the stance my father taught me, one of the guys made a sound like a bell ringing, and we went to it. I'll never forget. Dick came running at me, and he never stopped swinging and hitting and pushing 'til he knocked me down. I think he still wanted to keep hitting me. I'm not that dumb though, I stayed down and yelled to the guys to ring the bell so the round would be over. It was my last fight and I'm glad; at least my teeth are straight and not knocked out.

The Depression was in full flower about this time, so nobody talked about anything but money, or mostly the lack of it. Our parents sure got the word across to Dick and me as to what a sacrifice they were making to send us to college. When we finally arrived at school, it was so exciting, so different, and so much fun, we forgot to worry about sacrificing, and responsibility, and our duty and stuff. Boy, it was a ball and all so new.

Dick and I were rooming together. We were assigned to Freshman Hall, which was called the "cardboard palace." It was stucco on the outside, and very thin plywood board on the inside to separate rooms and things. Lights would go out at 10 p.m., and the building would be in complete darkness except for a small light in the common bathroom. You would have to grope down the hall to get there.

One of the guys next door to us snored. His bed was right next to Dick's except for a plywood dividing wall that did little to cut down the sound. So Dick told the kid who snored that he wanted him to share in a system he was developing. The system would tie into the electrical wires at a point where it wouldn't be affected by the master switch. We could have lights all night to study more and do better in class. The snoring kid was all for it. Since he was hell bent on becoming an electrical engineer, even as a freshman he was loaded with math. So a small hole was made in the area of the kid's wall in order to transfer the electrical wires from our room to his, the room of the snoring "engineer." That's what Dick *told* him (he was great with the gab) what he *did* was something else. He got a piece of glass tubing that was hollow inside, a gallon container of water, rubber hosing, and then he waited. The following night, when the engineer was snoring away like a steam locomotive, Dick stood on his bed, lifted the container of water and started a rite of passage with a steady stream of water swirling through the glass tubing, and coming out over the bed of his soon-to-be enemy. Snorers don't wake up easily. The noise went on and on, and the water suddenly was running out. Just in time, we heard the roar. With no lights available, the engineer couldn't know what in the hell was going on. Dick quietly removed the tubing and we went to sleep—with our door locked.

Well, that's what the priest rector called ungentlemanly conduct a few days later when he had us thrown out of Freshman Hall, and relegated to the school's dormitory, where Dick wound up sleeping with more than 20 snoring roommates. We could have been thrown out of school, but then the school would have had to give back the tuition money.

We also had the problem of Parent's Day coming up in a couple of weeks. You know, the parents who were making all those sacrifices. Well, resourceful old Dick went back to our former resident hall, and made a deal with a fellow freshman from Oregon whose parents weren't able to come for Parent's

Day, since it was too far. So, on Parent's Day, we used his room. He was a very neat person. Our parents were impressed with "our" room and with us.

We survived a South Bend winter. We used borrowed books to keep up with our studies and finally we welcomed the long-delayed spring. We enrolled for our sophomore year and were given a corner room in Ryan Hall. We hoped to have quiet neighbors. We had discovered that we weren't dormitory types.

ECLECTIC AND THE ELECTRIC TRAIN
1934

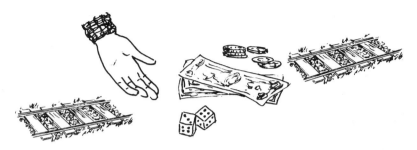

My roommate, Dick, and I were freshmen going home for a long weekend. It wasn't all that far, just 80 miles. Our homes were in Chicago, and we were attending the University of Notre Dame outside of South Bend, Indiana. Some people call Notre Dame a country school, not to be compared to city schools like the University of Chicago or Northwestern University. So much for them!

We were going to hitchhike home. There was the South Shore electric train we could ride, but we decided we would rather save our money and spend it when we got to Chicago—except we didn't have any money to save. We'd spent our last bit of change on the trolley that took us to the edge of South Bend where the two-lane highway to Chicago was located. The weather was cloudy and turning cold. There were about 25 other students all waiting for a free lift to Chicago. Times were different then—the roads were narrow and rough, but people were friendly and unafraid. It was fun for them to pick up a college kid or two and talk with them during the trip. Dick and I made our usual dime bet on who would be picked up first—singles had a better chance of getting a ride than two guys. We didn't have the dime to bet, but we were roommates and we kept accounts.

We may have been broke, but at least we weren't hungry. In the dining hall where all the students ate at tables for ten, they served us hot apple pie for dessert that day. All our food came from farms that surrounded the school as far as the eye could see. The farms were run by the Holy Cross brothers, and the school was run by the Holy Cross priests. There was never a shortage of food, all fresh from the farm. You could put a slice of cheese on your hot apple pie if that's what you wanted, or you could cut a slice of butter from the brick-sized pounds located at either end of your table. The pie was hot, and the butter a melting delight. The football types would cut themselves a *slab* of butter. When we did get home at this first semester break, our folks were over-joyed to see us—they were making great sacrifices to provide us with college educations, which they weren't privileged to have had and knew little about. Notre Dame was a great school, their sons had gained 10 pounds during the first semester. How about that!

Back on the highway, I won and was picked up before Dick. Believe it or not I got into a brand new "Model T" Ford. They were Henry Ford's first and the country's only sedans. They were all painted black and had three pedals on the floor—one to go forward, one to go backwards, and the third to brake the car to a stop. The gas throttle was on the side of the steering wheel. The cars were started with a crank inserted at the front of the motor and turned to make the motor start. If the motor backfired while it was being started, look out for your wrist. By this time, the Model T had long been replaced by later and more advanced cars. This brand new Model T was from a stock pile in Detroit reserved for Ford dealers to buy. This one would be a Christmas present from a dealer to his son. There was limited speed and no heater, but we did keep moving along. I wondered if Dick had gotten a ride. When the "tin Lizzie," as the early Fords were called, got to Gary, Indiana, a little over half way home, I was unaware that we had left the highway which went through town and made lots of turns.

Finally the man driving, an employee who was delivering the car to his boss said, "End of the line, fellow." I got out to discover I was at the other end of town, far from the highway. Hitching a ride back to the highway would be a major problem. However, there was a traffic light close by. I stood near it and when traffic stopped I tried to talk myself into a ride. Time passed, the light turned green, the light turned red. When the light turned red the last time, a large white hearse stopped, and while the light was red the driver got out of his driver's seat, went around to the back and opened the wide door that was used for caskets. Dick got out! We stayed together and reached home six hours and five lifts later. When it got dark, I didn't think we would ever make it, and by then there was also a large hole where the apple pie used to be. When the weekend was over, our parents ordered us back to school by train.

This thing about money or the lack of it was a constant problem for me and for my folks who were paying for two of us to go to college. In my sophomore year, I got carried away. I was feeling lonesome for family and I wrote to my folks and told them how much I appreciated being at Notre Dame, and how I didn't want it to be such a burden on them. Then I told them if they wanted to cut my monthly allowance (a pittance) of four dollars and a half, it was okay by me. They did! And it wasn't a bit okay by me. I stopped getting lonesome after that!

During meals in the dining hall, there was a game where you could make money. The dining tables were oak and had a highly polished finish. The object of the game was to slide a salt or pepper shaker across the table and have it stop, leaning over the edge of the table, but not falling off. It took practice and finesse. I preferred to use my brain. When I sat down to play with freshmen or rich kids from South America, I would shake salt into my hand and then, unnoticed, put the stuff in my mouth. If it was too sticky a mess, I would add a sip of water—the salt melted and I would wet a finger and then rub it on the table, an inch or two from the edge. You couldn't see anything but it sure put a stop to your opponent's salt shaker when he slid it across the table. If he slid it faster and it went across the salt barrier, that much force would send it off the edge of the table. I liked the money I won, but I worried about the mess of salt I swallowed, and what it would do to my irrigation system.

At Christmas time, I went home on the same train as my brother. When he was around, he was always taking care of me—I think my father had told him to. Anyway, the seniors played craps on the train, a dice game that required luck and skill. Well, I'm left-handed. The nuns used a ruler to help me learn to write with my right hand. I think they said the devil was left-handed—all I knew was if I rolled the dice with my left hand, and called on the devil for help while doing it, things worked out just fine. On the train ride home, I hunkered around those old men seniors and pretty soon started to bet. The devil and my left hand were in good form. Wouldn't you know, my older brother showed up at the little smoking area on the train where the game was being played. He gave me *the look*! I had seen that look all my life. It meant come here, right now. I smiled back and played on. In a couple of minutes, he was back.

This time he called out, "Bob, the train's slowing up for 63rd Street." Sixty-third is where we got off—so I picked up my money which used to belong to those seniors and left with my brother.

In the vestibule between cars he told me if those guys knew I wasn't a senior, there would be hell to pay. "It won't be long," he said, "before they show up."

"So why worry," I said, "we're getting off the train."

"Not yet," he said, "I used that to get you out of the card game."

Holy Christopher, where could I hide on a four-car electric passenger train? So I said, "Here, you take the money and I'll let them kick me around."

He wasn't interested. I don't know what it is about big brothers. Then I thought, maybe the game is going on and no one's gotten wise to us. I wasn't too sure about that. Anyway, we were in the vestibule and the train was making a stop, not our stop, but who wants to die a hero? When the doors opened, I said so long to my brother and I got out. That was about enough for one day, so I hailed a cab. When I told him where my home was, he wanted to see the money before we made the trip. I just had enough. Anyway, I beat my brother home. I won that one.

The Glow of Embers

56

THE ICE CAPADE
1936

Kennedy, Coyle, my roommate Dick, and I had finished a highly competitive two-man-team touch football game. We had found a field on the other side of St. Mary's lake where the Notre Dame campus drifted into the Holy Cross farms (our source of food). Coyle and I had won. Dick was let down—Kennedy should have caught Dick's passes, even if some of them landed a half block away from where he was running. So he did his "Dick thing"—he would race anyone across the frozen St. Mary's lake, a distance of about a good block. No one showed the slightest interest. Kennedy and Coyle walked around the lake while I stayed with my roomie, Dick, and tried to talk him out of proving something by running across the lake. He told me I was less than a man, and other things, but I turned down the invitation to run with him. It was getting colder by the minute. I thought I had convinced him of the folly of his proposal, and we'd forget everything, but I was wrong. All of a sudden he started from the shore. His first step went through the ice at the shore line where the ice was thinnest, but his second step put him on sound ice and he was on his way.

Kennedy and Coyle were half-way around the lake when I called to them. We all watched Dick as best we could since it was getting dark, and much colder. All went well as he approached the other shore. Then there was a splash as he broke through thin ice. He got up and was about thigh deep in shattered ice and

57

water. Dick reached shore by himself, and Coyle and Kennedy started walking the two or three blocks back to the campus with him to our resident hall. I began running to catch up with them and also to keep warm. It was very cold now. By the time I had caught up to the three of them, Dick was down to a slow, stumbling walk—his wet clothes were icing up. We were making our way along a path through an orchard when I spotted an old iron-wheeled wheelbarrow. It looked a hundred years old, but the wheels still turned, and we loaded Dick into it. If Dick wasn't scared, and I'm not saying he wasn't, we were. We all pulled at the wheelbarrow and headed for the campus infirmary, instead of the Resident Hall. The nuns at the infirmary were quick to exchange the iced clothes for warm blankets. Kennedy, Coyle and I went on to the dining hall for dinner.

During the evening, we decided to walk over to the infirmary and see our erstwhile iceman. Dick was living it up—hot chocolate and cream cake. When a nun stopped by to look in on her patient, we heard from her about how Dick had tried to save the life of this little bird with a broken wing that had floundered on the ice. What a con artist!

THE SKIN GAME
1935

We were sophomores at Notre Dame. We had made it. First year had been a ball. Now it was time to get serious. Dick and I were both students in the School of Commerce and took identical courses. Dick would borrow and read the assignment for one course, and I would read the assignment for another course. We each took notes and then switched the notes. Dick called it efficiency.

This year we were going to *buy* our books. Our years at Notre Dame were those of the Depression era, so freshman year, when Dick saw the price they charged for books that had to be dull, he made up our minds. We could use the money better. Instead of buying books, we'd just drop into rooms along the hall and borrow the books. We even—mostly—returned them. Some of the guys would stop by our room to get some information, and while they were there, they'd steal their books back. Some of the studious types couldn't wait 'til we were through, and would come barging in, interrupting our studying and wanting their books.

Then there was the guy with a full set of books who always said, "Sure, take it." We found that some of his books had never been opened.

One of the most difficult times in that year was when a friend of ours had to leave school because of finances. We often thought if only he could get a job in South Bend, or if only the school had any student loan funds available, or if only his dad was able to keep his job, it wouldn't have to happen. For dedicated students this was a small death. We who stayed on had a chance to see how lucky we were.

We were determined to give up bridge for our sophomore year. It was a luxury to be sure, and a no-win situation. How it got started, I'll never know, but two of the priests on campus were bridge addicts. Well, so were we. We'd go to one of their rooms in the evening, deal the cards, and never even know when the lights-out switch had been thrown in the residence halls. Of course, the priests had electricity without interruption. As for the bridge game, the priests were better than we were, which might have had something to do with our being invited. The priests would have a drink or two, we would pour from a large urn of very strong coffee, and the game went on. It usually ended at midnight with them winning. However, there were exceptions. If we were ahead by some freak of fate—or good cards like aces and kings—the game would go on (3 a.m. one time) until the priest posted a modest plus score. Later in the year we caught on to this, so when we were ahead and wanted to return to our room, one of us gave a sign and we played badly until we were behind. When the game was over, one of the priests would take us to the front door of the residence hall where they lived. He would hail a security guard with a flashlight, who would accompany us to our hall, unlock the door, and let us in.

For a couple of months, at the start of our sophomore year, our room had a rancid, or maybe fetid smell. It stunk! Dick's uncle, a politician associated with Chicago's Democratic party, had been rewarded for his role in getting out the vote during an election the year before, and so was appointed head of the City Dog Pound. When Dick arrived at Notre Dame, he brought with him 12 dog skins which he nailed to the walls of our room. It was early fall so our window stayed wide open, even when it rained, since the pelts hadn't been cured. We had no visitors. I complained to Dick and then waited. He always had a plan. (When the weather turned cold and the heat was turned on, I was ready to abandon our room, my home away from home.) Something had to give—or go. It happened the next Saturday night. Dick had been over at Freshman Hall during the day. When he came back, I was told there would be a beer and craps game in our room that night. Beer was a no-no on campus. That night, sure enough, some wide-eyed freshmen showed up. There were soft drinks and potato chips available, and also some empty beer cans that Dick had picked up downtown. Dick told the freshmen that they were too late for the beer, but the dice were out, and the gambling began. I wasn't there, I was over at the library taking out some books, but mostly concentrating on the attractive supervisor at the front desk, one of the few young women on campus. I stayed on at the library, and did my studying of the supervisor. When I returned to our room, Dick had twenty-three dollars and the dog skins were gone. He had used them to cover his bets in lieu of money. Don't ask me how he did it, but somehow it had to do with fur skins being our country's early acceptable specie for exchange. In a month or so the smell was gone. In about six weeks, the scent of the aftershave lotion he had used to camouflage the smell had disappeared, too. I'm glad I wasn't there that night, I might have wound up with one of those dog skins myself. Dick could make anything look like a good deal.

The Glow of Embers

JALOPY
1936

My junior year at Notre Dame was also the year of my holiness. The conscience always has been an exquisitely sensitive and perverse part of Irish life. It constantly has had to be shriven or you would remain tormented. A "black rober" could do this for you in his little box and somehow give you a blessing for your badness. One time while I was at Notre Dame, I wanted to be made as pure as the driven snow, and the confessor suggested that if I gave some time to the St. Vincent de Paul Society on campus I would have less time for "the trouble." The Society helped guide South Bend parishes in a variety of ways. They collected cast-off clothes from students, or anything else of value they chose to give, and arranged for it to get to the poor of South Bend. So it turned out that I went over and paid the Society a visit and learned about the other services they provided.

My assignment for the Society was to form, instruct, and coach a parish basketball team. My own qualifications for doing this was that I had been a member of Notre Dame's freshman basketball team (barely, and with no future). The parish was old, and the gymnasium, a part of their school, was ancient and unused. It was, let us say, a challenge. The good part was the enthusiasm of the young high-school-age boys about having a team of their own and playing in the Catholic Youth Organization's basketball league (known as CYO). The boys and the volunteer janitor for the parish cleaned up the gym. I bought new nets for the baskets and we were on our way.

My CYO team won a few games its first year—well, a couple (in fact, only one). The pastor of the parish was a basketball nut and would go out to the campus to watch the Notre Dame basketball team practice. He even told members of the team they could use his gym (our gym) whenever they wished. A couple of nights later, some of the team showed up. Imagine going to class in the morning, practicing basketball all afternoon, and then coming down to this old wreck of a building and running us off our court (Notre Dame has such dedicated student athletes). It was at this time that a Holy Cross priest, a member of the order that taught at Notre Dame, discovered synthetic rubber. So science was challenging sports, and now Notre Dame was to go forward on two fronts.

Students, even rich ones, were not allowed to have cars at Notre Dame. (In 1935, the captain of the Notre Dame football team, named O'Neill, backed his family's car a matter of fifteen feet to a better location while his family was visiting him on campus. It was reported, though hard to believe, that as a result he had to sit out the first game of the year.) The St. Vincent de Paul Society had been given an old jalopy and it still ran. I volunteered to be their designated chauffeur and was given permission to drive it on campus, off campus, wherever it served the Society's needs. I could drive it to basketball practice in South Bend and back onto the campus. Dick couldn't make up his mind whether I was to be called "rev" for reverend because of the St. Vincent post, or "coach" because of the basketball post.

My St. Vincent de Paul work wasn't all fun and games either; it had another side. The director in charge of the Society's work called me in one day, explained a serious problem and asked me for help. I was told to go to the poorest part of South Bend and visit a woman. In case she was desperate for food, I was given $5.00 and authorized to buy some. What my director was really interested in and wanted to know, however, was whether that lady was receiving birth control advice and things from a local government agency. Such information and devices were against the law. This sort of situation was all kind of new to me, and I swallowed. (I couldn't even talk to girls without blushing.) I thought of my old jalopy and the prestige that it gave me on campus, and said I would try. I went to visit the woman at her home. It was a very poor home. I looked important, and so the lady of the house was very accepting of my being there. She was giving her baby a bottle at the time, and the bottle contained only weak coffee. I excused myself and left for the grocery store. When I returned with milk and food, the woman was surprised and pleased. So I ventured into deep waters where I had never been before, and asked my questions. She was hesitant to reply. I had tried my best not to be explicit. She finally asked what would happen to her if she told me—would she go to jail? I said I didn't think so. (Darn that jalopy, I didn't want it this much.) Finally, she told me she had received information about what she should do, and also some prophylactic material for her to use. She had thrown whatever it was away—she didn't believe in it. The contraband that I had been talking about was not really a part of the government's program. It was being distributed by government employees whose own religious or moral views approved of it. That afternoon, Notre Dame and the St. Vincent de Paul Society had provided me and my jalopy with an opportunity to grow up a little; moreover, I've never forgotten it. The way it worked out, I was still not off the hook. The director had also said that if I found the government agency people were indeed involved, I was to go to downtown South Bend and report this to B. Varga. He was a government employee sympathetic to our side of the issue.

The jalopy and I headed to town. I tethered it outside and entered the agency building alone. I asked a man at the desk to see Mr. B. Varga. He pointed to a desk that had a name plate in front. It said "Barbara Varga," and she was sitting there, only a few years older than I was. I swallowed and I gulped, and I didn't want to go near her, but I did. As it happened, I found out later, she knew what was up and was reluctantly involved. She was very nice to me. It seems my SVDP director, Vincent McAloon, had set me up. I don't know why he did it, but I think it might have had something to do with my being a brash young man caught up in myself, with my jalopy, my basketball team, and glibness all over. The director thought that waking me up might help. As it worked out, Dick and I visited that mother every couple of months for the rest of the time we were at Notre Dame, and brought what food we could to her. Dick did the scrounging to get the food, borrowed a dress of his sister's for the mother, and found Christmas presents for the children. He also kept after me and the jalopy so we didn't miss a visit. We were a team.

Richard J. Carroll
1914–1945

Richard J. Carroll, Dick (my Notre Dame roommate named "shoelaces" by my mom), was a member of our group of four, and a Notre Dame graduate. A P38 pilot, he escorted Eisenhower's plane to Africa during World War II, and on a later mission was shot down in the desert. He landed intact, and was plenty thirsty by the time he was captured by the Italian forces. That desert was big, and hot, and lonesome. Later, as he was being taken to Italy across the Mediterranean Sea in an Italian submarine, against war rules—what rules (?)—our Navy caught up with them. The Italian sub was outmatched, surfaced, and released the crew and prisoners to fend for themselves. It was night and, from a safe distance, our forces shelled the sub, a sitting duck wallowing in the sea. Dick was an excellent swimmer and former lifeguard, but swimming away from shells doesn't work. So, unwittingly, our Navy killed one of our Army pilots that night in the Mediterranean Sea.

The Glow of Embers

MAC—ANOTHER DIMENSION
1911–

♪♪ CHIRH CHIRU FORU ♪♪
ODA NOTURE DAMU ♪♪

CHEER CHEER FOR OLD NOTRE DAME

Vincent McAloon, this strange little man called Mac, must have a pact with God. (I hope God knows about it.) He comes from a rich family in the east. One of the family's business interests was a funeral home which owned a large yacht. The yacht was used to transport remains for burial either to or from an offshore island. Mac's early education was in a seminary, and later he came to Notre Dame.

His mother said he started doing things for others when he was three. When he was older, he turned his sights on people in trouble. In time, he even tried to help those most resourceful of people, Gypsies. He might have been poorer for the effort, but the Gypsies discovered he had nothing for them to steal. He usually found someone who needed whatever he had more than he did. He had entered the seminary feeling that he could be of greater help to those in need. The discipline that was demanded in the seminary seemed to him a vast waste of time. (The military is also great for that "don't think, just obey" business.) His family wondered at this different young man who was always happy and always broke. That was to be his life.

At Notre Dame, Mac espoused the poor who lived next to the campus, most of whom were employed by the university at niggardly wages. His master's thesis was an eloquent statement drawing the contradiction between the courses being taught at the school concerning principles of social justice, and the same institution's practice of ignoring these principles. The university isn't being faulted here, it was trying desperately to survive through the worldwide Depression that closed so many other schools. Principles are best adhered to when survival is not being stalked. However, Mac wouldn't back down on a word of it, not even for his good friend and admirer, Father John O'Hara, President of Notre Dame. Mac stayed on at the school after graduation to direct the St. Vincent de Paul Society (a charitable organization) for a pittance.

During his school years at Notre Dame, Mac gathered a coterie of eight or ten students and offered us an opportunity to live a life of poverty with him. Since our parents could afford to send us away to college, such a change in our lives would be quite difficult. We students were young. We were the kind of people who volunteered to go to war to save humanity; we were generous, apostolic and—God knows—*naive*. A couple of years down the pike, after we were graduated, Mac sounded the clarion call. We were to take over a high school that was being run by the Benedictine Order about 70 miles south of Chicago. Our leader, Mac, had convinced the Benedictines that teaching wasn't their historic calling; better that they should stick to works of mercy and a continuing deep study of God and His world. Our taking over the teaching in the high school, however, didn't work out. By that time, most of us were involved with becoming doctors or lawyers, or were enmeshed in family businesses. My own response was to send a picture of a young lady I hoped to wed and provide for. The teaching recompense we would have received couldn't have sustained a single person without help from home. When you're young, you can spend lots of time plotting a future and making plans for yourself that turn out to be pie in the sky.

I remember the year after I left school, I was working in the area of South Bend, Indiana, where Notre Dame is located. I stopped over to see Mac. He asked a favor. His mother was coming to visit him. He had borrowed some of the clothing that the students at Notre Dame donated each year to the St. Vincent de Paul Society. He looked good compared to the way I was accustomed to seeing him during my school years when he dressed in clean rags. What he wanted from me was the use of my car for a day. For years he had written to his mother trying to explain this strange dedication to a life of poverty and living to help the poor. She had the resources to be of help, but whatever gifts she sent him were given away. She was on a trip across the country and planned to visit with Mac for a day. It would be good if she would get to see her son as a successful poor man with nice clothes and a car. It would please her.

It's hard to understand a person like Mac. You might find people like him in religious orders, but Mac was a total man of the world dedicating himself to the poor. The car, the spruced-up clothing, and some money I forced on him to be spent on treating his mother were all part of a charade for her sake. (Why allow her to view her son as a nothing, and break her heart?) It was all done as a kindness to the mother he loved. It would offset the illusion she had of her son starving to death while contradicting the principle of prudent management of one's resources which meant so much in her own life.

In time I forgot about Mac, but he didn't forget about me. He showed up some years later at my home and met my wife. Mac had served in the Army during World War II. He entered as a private and held on to that status for the remainder of the war. He wasn't a war enthusiast. When his company had a correspondent take a picture of them, Mac was up front, the only one in a clean white shirt, probably standing so his mother could see it was him. She could show it to her friends and tell them he was much neater and cleaner than those other scruffs. He would, of course, have been a sniper's delight if his company ever got close to the front line. None of the other platoons, however, seemed interested in this group as an asset. So they just kept a low profile—cleaning latrines, peeling potatoes, and doing odd jobs. His company was one of the first sent home when the Germans accepted defeat.

Mac wasn't home for long. It seems he had fallen in love with Rome and the Italians and was anxious to return there to help his fellow man. He was visiting with us on his way back to Europe. He stayed around a few days, beginning a lawn and flower garden to beautify our backyard; he also baby-sat our daughters while Mary, my lovely young bride, produced the first of what turned out to be three sons. Mary had come to love this fellow and entrusted her small daughters to his antics and care. She actually offered to have him name this first baby boy. He chose Christopher.

When Mac left our house for Rome, he hitchhiked. He promised he wouldn't give away any of the money we gave him, but would use it for food and a place to stay. There are a lot of Franciscan friaries across the United States, and already the word of this young man's dedication and work for the poor had spread. He would be welcomed anywhere by the Franciscans with open arms. The Franciscans have, for centuries, kept their kitchen doors open for wayfarers.

Mac had an older brother living in the east who cared about him, and when he heard Mac was on his way to Rome this brother got him passage on a freighter. (I wonder if Mac had intended to walk around the Atlantic Ocean to get there.) The freighter landed in Portugal, where Mac gave what money he had left to an orphan's home and began his trek to Rome. Mac thought that if things got tough while walking across Portugal and Spain, he could always locate a Franciscan house and head for the kitchen door. It didn't work out as well as he expected. He was after all, an American. Americans had won the war without anyone being killed at home, so even the generous Franciscans had a hard time giving even reluctant hospitality to a person born and raised in the land of the free and the rich. Mac was never discouraged. He would persist once he'd made up his mind. (Maybe he and God *had* worked out a deal.) Anyway, he made it to Rome, and Rome had not been destroyed.

At this time in Rome, there was a Bishop Carroll from the states. It was said of the Bishop that he was burning the candle at both ends. He tried to do so much, but his constitution was fragile. He had met Mac when he was at Notre Dame, and they had enjoyed a friendship. So what do you know—the war was over and thousands of American soldiers wanted to see Europe before returning home. The United States government, through the USO (United Service Organization), asked Bishop Carroll if he would head the welcoming organization to accommodate Catholics and others who were coming to see Rome. Our government doesn't do things in a small way, so Bishop Carroll had a lot of planning to do. One of his projects was to have a large eating and gathering place where travelers could congregate, have something to eat, make plans for a night's lodging, and all those other things the USO has continued to provide right up to this day. Well, the Bishop looked around, but he didn't have to look too far. He remembered the ingenuity of this young friend of his from Notre Dame days, and he placed Mac in charge of the whole operation. I'm sure some visitors to Rome will remember the USO Center, for it was situated in a prominent corner approaching St. Peter's Basilica. The operation was large, it was noisy, it had food, souvenirs, relics, rosaries, and more. It was right for its time, and Mac had a ball. It served tons of fettucini and *vino* every day. A year or so later, when it was going full force, Mac asked to be replaced. Bishop Carroll was no longer around. The Bishop's candle had burned out at both ends.

Mac, the veteran, had kept in touch with the Army and his division. He had heard that a distraught and discouraged minister who was serving as chaplain at Okinawa had abandoned his post. The minister was assisted by others in being stowed on a transport back to the states. The Army could find no replacement. Those Pacific Islands were beyond the end of the world after the end of the war. To think of Okinawa is to forget the Bali Hai of *South Pacific.* Okinawa was a living disaster with a shattered people, a junkyard of broken ships, smashed tanks, and the remnants of downed planes. It was no place anyone wanted to be. There was nothing to do, nowhere to go under a relentless sun. So Mac took the assignment. He wasn't a cleric, but he was the only one who volunteered.

On his way to Okinawa, he stopped by once again to visit us in our home in Chicago, with the hope that he'd get to name another child. Our third son is Paul Vincent. Vincent is Mac's middle name. A couple of days, and he was on his way—not a *padre*, but the best the Army could offer its people on Okinawa. Mac knew all about the different services: Jewish, Protestant, Catholic, and Buddhist. Everyone could get a little help. Two years later, the Army notified the commanding officer they had found an ordained religious man, a chaplain, who was being assigned to the island to relieve Mac.

So Mac's assignment on Okinawa was over. He went back to Rome to his original apostolate, teaching in a high school designed for the children of diplomats. It was run by the same order of priests who are at Notre Dame. Mac's *pensione* was nearby, four stories up a stairway right under the roof. It was his private place. (I don't know of anyone who ever visited him there. Maybe God did!) Teaching was a joy for Mac and for his students. He was great for fun and games while also teaching discipline, showing the students how to see self-discipline as a plus in their lives to understand and practice.

While in Rome, Mac met a man who owned a restaurant in the downtown area, as well as an adjoining building built of stone which was hundreds of years old. Mac and *il trattore* worked out a deal. Two good-sized rooms in the stone building were given to Mac to use. There he opened the Notre Dame Club of Rome. The Notre Dame alumni loved to travel, especially to Rome. They came in droves. They were greeted with hospitality and a glass of wine in the stone rooms, and then welcomed into the *trattoria* next door where they dined. That *trattoria* was called Scoglio di Frisio, and Mac was in charge of the dining room there. He was both *maggiordomo* and master of ceremonies. He taught the

Americans to sing their school song in Italian, and then he would turn to the five-piece Italian band and help them to sing the same song in English.

Father Hesburgh, Notre Dame's longtime president, was just one of the famous people who visited with Mac at the Club. A few years later I got over there to see the end of this arrangement. The *trattoria* had been sold and there would no longer be reciprocity with Mac and the use of the stone building. Mary and I had dinner at that *trattoria* a few days before Mac completed his commitment. It still had a dominant clientele, although this time it wasn't the Irish and their fellow Americans. The new owner, by contract, supplied food and wine at two seatings. By arrangement, twice a night on each day of the year, buses pulled up to the entrance and unloaded the new diners. They were all Japanese. When Mary and I, our daughter Carol and her husband Bill were there, we were the only non-Japanese among the patrons. The master of ceremonies, still our friend Mac, did his best—the Japanese all helping him with their language, and he helping them to learn how to sing the Notre Dame Victory March. It was mayhem!

During the Persian Gulf War, the school where Mac taught was closed. The authorities decided not to open it again. The University of Notre Dame, seeing Mac was growing old (83), invited him home and honored him at a banquet on campus. They asked if he would like to come and live there as a guest of the school.

If you should happen to visit Notre Dame, he's the one who's conducting the walking tours through the school's Basilica. If you wish to show your thanks with a gratuity, he'll show you to the poor box.

The Glow of Embers

Along the Way

Along the Way

When the shutter on a camera opens one can see, for a brief moment, poignant memories from the past. So too, in the dark of night when half awake, images of other times return. These fragments are recalled in Along the Way.

BUNNY AND THE SIDE OF THE MOUNTAIN

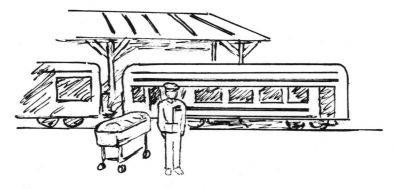

He was called Bunny. He had four brothers and two sisters. Bunny played high school football before going to college at Notre Dame. When the high school season was over, his father gave a dinner for the whole team—coaches and all—at the country club. The Veeneman family had come from Kentucky; the father was a whisky-producing heir. They lived in a large apartment, large enough to include a live-in Japanese couple to do the chores. When Bunny's sister, Mary, would be sent to the grocery store with her little red wagon to buy the family's food, she would always stop at Walgreen's drug store on her way home. There at the end of the soda fountain, sitting on a stool was the neighborhood bookie. He liked Mary, but more than that, he liked the fact that her mother was a heavy bettor.

At their large apartment building, there was an English basement on the lower level where we played great ping-pong. The sweaty winners won free milk-shakes. In every way, we lived the good life. In time, we all went away to college and before we knew it we were ready to go out and start life on our own.

The young Veenemans wasted no time in getting married. I was master of ceremonies at each of their weddings, including Bunny's. I felt like a part of the family. When Bunny was married, it was in the cathedral, and then all of us were off to the country club for the reception—the father-of-the-bride's club.

Bunny's bride had an only sister who was maid of honor, and I was best man. It was quite a day for me. The bride's sister was vivacious, a beauty, and she liked to kiss. Well, there was champagne and a lot of kissing all around. My wife attended the wedding—I never did ask her what she thought.

At this time the country was moving closer to World War II. Bunny had joined the Marines as a flyer. Man, he looked good in a uniform! We were all young adults, we had our great health and the future belonged to us, or so we thought.

Things began to happen a few months later. About four o'clock one morning, I received a phone call. Bunny had been on a practice bombing mission in California, had failed to come out of a dive, and ended his life on the side of a mountain. The family accepted it as best they could.

At the time of the tragedy, the bride's parents were in Florida enjoying a winter vacation. Also about this time, John L. Lewis, head of the coal union was defying the President with a coal strike curtailing steam-driven passenger trains from running. That was why the bride's parents couldn't get back to Chicago for the funeral.

The body, or what there was of it, was given priority, put on a train, and brought from the West Coast. When the train arrived in Chicago early one morning, we were all at the station to receive it. It was a sorry time. The Marines had sent one of their own to accompany the remains. He was a be-medaled, be-ribbon-ed, straight-standing, handsome young Marine officer just about Bunny's age. *He* met the group—Bunny's family, the bride and her sister and then led the local Marine unit as it accompanied the casket to the hearse. The next two days were hectic. Bunny had so many friends, plus extended family from Kentucky, and the bride had local relatives and friends. There was High Mass, and after that the body was interred.

The next morning Bunny's father phoned. By this time he had depleted much of his fortune. He no longer employed the Japanese couple, and the bets placed at Walgreen's were much smaller. He invited me to attend a family dinner that evening at the country club. I didn't think he could afford it, but what was I to say—I accepted his invitation. He also said that the bride's parents had driven from Florida, arriving the night before. The father was too tired to go out, but the mother would be with us.

That evening, in good southern fashion, we started with cocktails. As I looked about the group, I was struck by the sight of the bride's mother. She looked awful. She almost seemed to be in shock. I felt so sorry for her. The meal was eventually served. Bunny's family carried on in a fashion that would have pleased him; they saw more in death than tragedy.

Before dessert was served, the bride's sister—my kissing friend on Bunny's wedding day—asked if she could see me for a moment alone. Her name was Cathy. I was delighted to oblige. We left the dining area and went to where we could be alone. She said she needed advice and so was coming to someone older (six years at most, as I recall). My ardor waned. This is what she told me: she and the handsome young Marine officer who had arrived two days before had talked it over, prayed about it, and had decided to get married. She showed me her left hand with a giant Marine ring held in place by a tiny handkerchief attached to her wrist. They were going to leave by train that night for California. He had his orders to return. What did I think? Was it all right? Well, I looked in her eyes and found the answer. A hundred-thousand horses couldn't have kept her from going. To have one daughter suffer such a loss, and have the other daughter leave so abruptly, it was easy to understand the mother's anguish and the father's inability to attend the dinner. That night, about midnight, the two of them left by train for California. They still live out west. It took! They have seven children!!

Bunny's death devastated his beautiful bride of six months. She never remarried.

James R. Veeneman
1919–1943

James R. Veeneman, called Bunny, died at the age of 24. He was graduated from the University of Notre Dame. He was a Marine dive-bomber pilot. On a night practice mission over California, his plane failed to come out of a dive and, on impact, ignited the side of a mountain. Pilots in the other planes he was practicing with called to him in vain. Feathers found in the wreckage suggested that a high flying bird may have crashed through the windshield of his plane.

HERM

Herman was called "Herm." The nickname brought you closer to this warm and friendly guy. His mother died when he was six years old. His father's only communication with him came from behind a newspaper, and mostly it was a grunt. Aunt Mary, Herm's father's unmarried older sister, came to the house to help with the chores. Besides doing those, she mostly spent the free time she had in her room with a rosary. She stayed for thirty years and then died quietly. Herm's younger sister Mary, coped with the loss of her mother as best she could by being slow to speak, a quiet presence. Herm's two older brothers handled it in their own way. Who knows?

Togetherness for the family happened once a year and was associated with their Christmas tree. Other than that, they were on their own—each with an independent life.

Though Herm was very young when his mother died, he never forgot her and much of his life was centered on that memory. I gather she had been the head, as well as the heart and warmth, of their family life. Herm's father worked for the park district and wore a leather jacket to work. He had about as much to say there as he did at home.

When I first met Herm, he had a paper route. In fact, at some point he took on a second route. He was, maybe, sixteen years old. He kept the route right through college where he earned an engineering degree. I sometimes thought of him in the winter when it was bitter cold or when it was raining, and I was warm and the bed was soft. Mechanical engineers as a rule are not the most scintillating people. They think logically, act mechanically, and rarely get upset. They are not great at making jokes. They're solid and controlled.

Herm was raised in a bungalow. On the side of the house, there was a concrete stairway with a narrow portico which led to the front entrance. A bedroom was next to this portico and its windows were tall. So we would climb the stairs, walk to the window which was never locked, and step into Herm's quarters. If it was Saturday morning, Herm would be sleeping after finishing his paper route. When he had those two newspaper routes, he would be up and delivering papers at four-thirty in the morning and he would get back home about eight. Even if Herm was out somewhere, it was our gathering place where we scrounged around. There was always food and stuff on the front window sill.

Herm never seemed to complain or ask anything of others. He was generous and kind and went out of his way to talk to people. He especially liked to talk to my mother whenever he visited with us. He so wanted her to like him, and she did.

With girls, Herm related directly. No fooling around or game playing. He was a guy and she was a girl, it was plain that's why they were together. Mostly, with girls, he was too obvious—they preferred to make a game of it. Herm was aggressive, yet he wasn't too forward. As far as most girls were concerned, he was just unromantic. With Dick, Jimmy, and the other guys, he was friendly, satisfied to have others lead, and solid as a rock as a friend. He was also strong as a lion, and captain of his college wrestling team.

One time I disappointed him. He was going to act out of character just to please me. It was at a Saturday evening wrestling contest with another university—he was going to lift his opponent and slam him to the mat. Such an act was *macho* (which was a negative word at that time). He would do it, however, in an effort to impress me, even though he knew such conduct would cause him to lose the respect of his coach and other members of his college team, as well as the opposition. He slammed his opponent, and I arrived too late to see the contest. I was driving and had no excuse. I don't think, even though he tried, Herm has ever forgiven me.

There were four of us who hung around together—Dick, Jimmy (who was called Bunny), Herm and myself. We finished high school together and went on to college. We all finished college, a year or so apart. World War II hadn't started, but plans were being made and it was only a matter of time. Boeing, the airplane manufacturer out on the west coast near San Diego, was combing the country trying to hire engineers. Their offer was attractive, plus California had mild weather year-round, and skiing on nearby mountains. Although not mentioned, such an offer meant that those workers would probably be deferred from military service. There would be overtime pay, and they would be 3,000 miles away from a bullet. If you think young people wanted to go to war to serve whatever and get killed in the process, you must live in another world. Of those four friends who comprised the group, two entered the service, and were killed. Herm and I were the ones who stayed home. Herm's job making war machines deferred him, and I suppose if we've come this far, I'd better tell about myself.

I was just married and, when I saw my draft number striding to the top of the heap, I enlisted in the Navy. I wanted to be a Navy flyer, mostly to wear one of those great looking navy-blue uniforms with a white shirt. So while waiting to be called up, I was drying dishes in our apartment one night with my lovely wife close by, when my ulcerous (unbeknownst to me) stomach blew out. There was lots of blood, and it was pretty scary. To illustrate the kind of driven character I was—which probably brought on my condition—not only did I insist on driving myself to the hospital, but I stopped on the way to tell my father (my boss) how to cover for me in my absence. I made it to the hospital—

just barely! They covered my body in ice (today it would be considered an Ice Age procedure), gave me a couple of blood transfusions, and told me at length what a damned fool I was, and how dumb as well. So that's how I missed the service and that great looking navy-blue uniform. The Navy wanted someone healthier and hopefully more intelligent. (It was a great act of contrition I made that night, probably my best. It's always smart to get on the right side.)

When he was graduated from engineering school, Herm signed a contract to work for Boeing. Before leaving for the west coast, however, he found a mate. Marie was an only child. She was strong-willed and anxious to leave home. She and her parents were miles apart about what she should do with her life. She would have none of it, so Herm was her way out. They were married in a small ceremony, her parents and a few friends attending, and then left to board a train for their honeymoon trip and life in California.

During the war, I would write an occasional letter to friends who were in the service, bringing them up to date on local happenings, and Herm was included. One day I received a letter from his wife, a strange letter which she wanted me to include in my war correspondence. She wrote about herself and her love of dogs. She had three and wished she had more. She mentioned that she thought they were so much better friends than babies could be. I didn't think Herm would agree, and I didn't include the letter. Within a year, she left Herm, joined one of the military services and made her career there. She asked for, and received, an overseas assignment. Her parents didn't hear from Marie about this change and were devastated to learn of it. Herm didn't hear from Marie again. When she left, she did not fault Herm, she just said goodbye and walked away. Herm never forgot the parents of his first wife, and gave them what succor he could. They seemed to have lost their daughter, although they wrote to her and phoned her. She had nothing to say. She never came home. It is the destiny of some to live their lives alone, friends only to themselves. A sad and secret life, but maybe for them their only choice.

So after a short marriage, Herm found himself alone once again. He still wanted a wife he could love, a wife for whom he could do all the nice kinds of things he had not been able to do for his own mother. Instead, he was alone and away from where he grew up. Herm was committed to his work contract with Boeing, and tried to adjust to a solitary existence. With his marriage dissolved, he decided to give up his apartment, and try to find a house where he could rent a room. This brief first marriage at least convinced him that he never wanted to live alone the way he grew up. In time, he heard of a family that was looking for someone who would rent their extra room and bath. It was the Nelsons. He gave up his apartment and took abode with Meg Nelson, who had four daughters, the oldest of whom was in her teens and four years younger than Herm.

Mrs. Nelson was a gracious landlord, and occasionally invited Herm to have dinner with the family. Besides his work, with overtime and all, Herm filled his life either playing sports or attending professional games. With the Nelsons, his life was better—he wasn't entirely alone.

Life was tranquil at the Nelsons. Then on September 23, a Saturday night, tranquility ended. Herm had worked overtime and had gotten home about eleven. He had gone to his room, shed his clothes, brushed his teeth, and laid down for a good night's sleep. It had been a long day and he needed this chance to rest. As it was Saturday night, San Diego was alive with sailor types who were ashore, lonesome, and looking for an antidote. Two who had over-imbibed decided to clear their heads with a walk around the neighborhood. At that particular time, Roberta, Mrs. Nelson's oldest daughter, left the home of her aunt where she had spent the evening, and began walking the short two and a half blocks home. She had been visiting with her favorite aunt with whom she had spent many an evening before. Halfway home she was hailed from across the street by the two imbibers. Roberta thought whoever was hailing her must know her either from work, or school, or church. She half waved her hand, then realizing that they were unknown to her, proceeded at an increased pace. She trotted, then ran, and got her key in the door lock by the time they caught up.

She opened the door and shouted, "Mother!" in a tone that would surely evoke a response.

It did. In the meantime, the young seamen were floundering around as if they were trying to keep their balance during a heavy sea. They were in the house and doing their best to get about their business. From the second floor landing, Mrs. Nelson knew what was up, but didn't know what to do. Men, even young men, can get so taken up, and time was of the essence.

She turned and rushed to Herm's closed door, rapped sharply, and called, "Herman, Herman!"

From somewhere far away, he slowly responded, got up, put on his bathrobe, and opened the door. Mrs. Nelson's look told him the story. Would he come and save the family honor? He would and he did.

Coming down to the front hall with his hands in his pockets, he said in a fatherly fashion still only half awake, "That's enough of this."

The seamen turned in unison, and the larger of the two launched a powerhouse right to the wrestling champ's nose. In a second, Herm became fully awake and then sank gently to the floor spreading blood copiously. The blood gave more than pause to the intruders who were last seen running in chaotic strides down the center of the street.

Herm was helped to his feet and was half carried, half led by mother and daughter to the kitchen. The bleeding was stopped with lots of ice and blood-splattered towels. At her mother's direction, Roberta made tea for Herm. This helped to distract Roberta from crying and having fits of hysteria.

It was a long night. The nose was one thing, but the surrounding area of Herm's face was turning black and blue like the face of a beaten boxer. Herm kept thinking over and over to himself why he hadn't tried to ward off the arm and given the gentleman a responding knee to his groin that would have put him into a state of ecstatic pain. Then he could have turned to the comrade in debauchery and broken his arms. He couldn't seem to accept the fact that at the time he was only half-awake. Mother, Roberta, and Herm all finally dispersed to their rooms and found time to rest. During the following days, Herm was proclaimed a hero by the Nelson family, by friends, and fellow workers. But his face was not quite that of a Hollywood hero.

Good comes from bad. Mrs. Nelson became a mother-in-law. Roberta became a bride, and the hero, Herm, became a groom. Most of San Diego's Swedish community were friends of Meg Nelson and they were present for the marriage of her oldest daughter. Herm never stopped smiling. He loved his Roberta and, at last, what he had so wished for was his.

AN IRANIAN FRIEND

Hushang Israeli was a small, ingratiating Iranian youth about sixteen years old. He was all smiles and acquiescence and was the most industrious young man I ever met. He knew few words of English. He was my brother's caddie. My brother wasn't playing good golf (even when he was, he groused like the world was going to end before he got to finish the round), so with his short fuse he was giving his "dumb" caddie Hushang a rough time. Hushang went on smiling, and nodding, and not understanding a word my brother said. So I suggested to my brother that we change caddies. I wanted to collect my bets if I beat him. The way it was, when the game was over, my brother would issue an official complaint, ream out the caddie master, and go looking for the club president—all in order to cancel paying the money he lost to me (seventy-five cents). My brother was a "principled" player, he not only held on to the principal, but wouldn't pay interest for delaying payment. Brothers are something else.

By the time the golf game was over, a grunting sign language communication had begun between Hushang and me. His career as a caddie could be short-lived, so I invited him to come to my house the next morning and clean windows, or some such chore. I wrote my address out for him, said goodbye and forgot about him. The way things happen always surprises me. At dinner that night, my wife Mary mentioned that spring had arrived and the windows of the house needed cleaning. She wondered where she could find a window cleaner. I'd had a cocktail or so, and never even thought about, or remembered, my Iranian acquaintance.

Well, the next morning, bright and early, there was Hushang sitting on the front steps quietly waiting. Two good things happened (really three—my wife was amazed at how I had found a window cleaner during the night!). The first of the good things: the windows were cleaned to a perfection that suited my wife, who is part German (her other part is French, I like the French better); and second, Hushang met Robert, our six-year-old son. I call him Bobby. When he grew up, he said he didn't mind if his *dad* called him Bobby. It was an implied threat to his brothers and sisters, or the rest of the world. Robert or Bob—okay—just don't say Bobby. Hushang stayed on to cut the lawn, plant flowers, clean the basement, and take handwritten lists to the local stores to pick up things for Mrs. Cronin. He was never idle— dishes were washed, carpets were vacuumed—everything in the house was clean and in running order. Much more important than this, however, was that he was learning English from the best of all teachers—a six-year-old Bobby. They did everything that summer together, and talked it all through. Bobby still had some baby colloquialisms, and sure enough we soon heard Hushang using them. They were two happy, close friends.

In the fall Bobby began school, and Hushang went away to a job of some sort. Things could have ended there, but they didn't. Shortly before Christmas, Hushang stopped by to see my wife. He had a suitcase filled with white Arrow shirts—a quality product. He was the door-to-door salesperson for a local haberdasher. (I got white shirts for Christmas.) Mary mentioned to our daughter, while Hushang was there, something about angora sweaters and, you guessed it, Hushang was back in a few days with all colors, all sizes, of angora sweaters—he had another contact. Soon our neighbors were buying from him—our smiling, ingratiating, hard-working Iranian friend. The English language continued to plague him and I noticed he had begun to stutter.

Hushang was a learning process for me. After a while, I discovered that he came from a well-to-do family. There was one Christmas time, while Hushang was in Chicago, that a present arrived for Mary from Hushang's family in Iran. It was a large, beautiful Persian rug. (It still is. I see it every time we're invited to dinner at our daughter Carol's house.) Hushang had an older brother here in the States, a graduate nuclear engineer, and he had an older sister studying law, so it wasn't surprising to me when Hushang said he was going away. He entered Ball State University in southern Indiana to study engineering. We said goodbye. If he could make it to Chicago for Christmas, Mary invited him to join us for dinner. (If he did come, the house would get a free cleaning, to boot.) He didn't make it for Christmas, and it wasn't 'til springtime that I received a phone call from a doctor. He asked if I knew Hushang Israeli. When I explained that my whole family knew him, he told me we might be able to help. Hushang was in a Chicago hospital and mute. He was unable to talk. The hospital staff had worked hard to get the name Cronin. We weren't the first Cronin the doctor had called. So I asked how we could help. The doctor wasn't sure. He would be in touch. At dinner that night, I mentioned the doctor's phone call to my wife Mary.

For a moment no one spoke, and then Bobby said in a small voice, "He'll talk to me." And that's what happened. That stutter Hushang developed was centered on fear, vocal fear. It ended up as an hysteria.

Bobby walked into that hospital room, and said, "Hello Hush." Hushang smiled and slowly started to talk.

Therapy followed. Everything takes time. Hushang returned to Ball State and graduated with a degree in engineering. This story's just beginning but it's not a story, it's the truth.

In Iran, the Shah reigned supreme. Iran was his. Oil flowed to the United States. The Shah was handsome; and in the United States, Jackie, President Kennedy's wife, was beloved around the world. Life was good. Hushang was invited, maybe instructed, to come back to Iran. You're probably wondering who paid for his education, and his private room in the hospital; maybe his family, maybe the Iranian State—I never knew. In either case, he left for home.

During the Shah's reign, Hushang worked as a mechanical engineer for the Shah, getting those tankers of oil out to the U.S. on time. There came a time when Hushang became sick and needed an operation. He made the trip to Chicago, stayed at the Drake Hotel, and went on to Mayo to be made whole again. That young man had come one long way. He returned to Iran for what in time turned out to be the end of the Shah's rule.

For at least the last twenty years, we have received at Christmas, from here or abroad, a card from Hushang thanking us again for our kindnesses. The cards from Iran were ornate, and his story of life was on a grand scale. The Shah, during one of these years, celebrated an important date—the 2,000th anniversary of Persia. Leaders around the world were invited by the Shah to be his guest. Great celebrating was planned. Mary and I were invited by Hushang to attend as his guests. We needed nothing, he would take care of everything. We would meet the Shah, and attend the official dinner. He reinforced his written invitation with a phone call. We're sorry we didn't go, we should have. It turned out to be the last hurrah for the Shah. He ended up without a homeland, a pathetic figure traveling from country to country.

When the revolution in Iran took place, we worried for Hushang and his family, but they got out of Iran and went to California where Hushang was stopped by the Pacific Ocean from going further. Had he stayed in Iran like other friends of the Shah, his life would have been over. Who needs an oil engineer when the oil isn't going anywhere?

It's time to meet Elyasse Houshang Bromandi, an American citizen who lives in California, buys and sells property, and continues to send the Cronins a Christmas card each year. I'll have to ask him the next time I get to California if his whole family changed their names.

During the summer of 1994, Hushang came to Chicago to visit Iranian relatives. He called and asked if he could come and visit with us. We were pleased. When he arrived, following him into the apartment in proper Muslim custom was a beautiful Iranian woman; she was his wife and the mother of their three children. Her English, her clothes, and her manners were impeccable. Hushang had done it again. This was my little caddie of close to forty years before. He still had the ingratiating smile, and a heart full of love for Mary and myself. We gave him Bobby's phone number, but Hushang didn't think Bobby would remember him. Hushang went on to tell us that while visiting Chicago, he had gone around to see if he could buy some gas stations. Gas stations were closing in Chicago. I couldn't understand buying them to be a good investment. My wife gave me the family *look* which meant: forget the business talk and join in entertaining our guests! And that was a joy—since Hushang's wife was such a beauty. Later, Hushang mentioned that the real estate business in California had gone into a funk, and he was looking elsewhere. He said he had an idea for gas stations that would make money. I never got to find out, but I'm more than inclined to believe his idea could work.

When we said goodbye, this boy-man-friend hugged me, wiping tears from his eyes. He's back in California, probably reviving the real estate market. If anyone could, it would be Hushang.

The Glow of Embers

JACK

"He wouldn't mind, if that's what you'd like to do—go ahead, call him Monsignor," I said.

Jack wouldn't mind (I mean, Monsignor). The Chancellor of the Archdiocese had recently brought the appointment back from Rome. It was during the early 1950s. The title would take time to get used to. Even Jack's mother slipped up once.

What's in a name? You'd better believe, ecclesiastically it's clout. Imagine being called "Pope," now that's a name! In a little while, we all forgot about his new title, "Monsignor," and went back to calling him Jack.

Jack was a priest, a good one, one of the best. He'd come from a home of Irish discipline, one with great respect for authority. His father was a streetcar motorman, and the only one who turned up for work during the height of a winter blizzard when Chicago was totally shut down by five feet of snow. And his father wasn't late getting to work either, even though it took two hours slogging his way through new blown snow. "Ours is not to reason why," said the Light Brigade charger.

Jack grew up and in due time, having made his choice, entered the seminary. He took his priestly vows, and started out to change everything—well, at least what he thought was wrong. I wonder what his father would think of that, were he alive!

Jack was small of stature with a giant heart. At times of confrontation, he seemed to grow taller. It was an exhilarating experience for him whenever the news media got involved. Jack made things happen on his own, but it wasn't easy. He made enemies along the way. God knows the Irish like to be loved on a large scale. Just take politics, where they excel. It's great when they walk into a hall cheered and respected. But let's face it, there are also those who hate their guts. It's no fun for the Irish to be hated—until they get used to it, and bash back—that's Irish politics. Jack learned he didn't have to be loved, but he did have to be right; and when he was right, he had to be strong in those things he stood for. Often enough, during his priesthood, what Jack stood for was at odds with the official policy of his employer, the Archdiocese.

Jack was made Monsignor while still a young priest. The Archdiocese protected and promoted his career. His assignment was to organize the laity so they could become a working force in the Church. The thought of an emerging young, well-educated laity having anything worthwhile to say or do would be the challenge for change. Many older members of the church were reluctant to accept this young, dynamic upstart—to put it mildly. Change went forward during the tenure of two cardinals, and when the office of cardinal became open for a third time, there was an extended period of search for a successor. It was during this interval that Jack moved into the political arena taking a strong stand against high-rise tenements. As Jack saw it, they were dead wrong for families. His position was at odds with the Democratic regime running the city. Since Jack was an espoused liberal Democrat, he became a political maverick. He was controversial, and he was having his say on the TV evening news programs. (It's now fifty year later, and across the country these high-rise abominations are being blasted to the ground by the government that created them.)

So there came a third cardinal and Jack was summarily put out to pasture. He wasn't the only clergyman to feel the heavy hand, but he was the most public one. Jack was assigned to Presentation Parish in a desperately poor neighborhood. City building inspectors, all good Democrats, descended upon the premises demanding new boilers, extensive plumbing and roof replacement. (So much for messing with the City's political system.) The nuns, elated with Jack's assignment to their parish, also needed their convent overhauled—at once!

What did Jack do? First he turned to those lay Catholics from the city and the suburbs who were looking for a way to be more active in their church. Priests from inside and outside the diocese also responded and overflowed the rectory. For the older parishioners, it was like a second coming; for others, it was akin to a Barnum & Bailey three-ring circus. When the lights came on and the show began, the Archdiocese looked the other way. Jack was ignored by his cardinal and by the institution he worked for. To a dedicated Irish priest, that was heartbreaking. It was also health-breaking, for before he was assigned to that parish he had already had one full-blown heart attack. Jack was aware of all this, but he was a priest and he would continue to do what he was called upon to do. When Presentation Parish was back on its feet, Jack was worn out. The struggle had taken its toll.

About this time one summer afternoon, a plane was en route from New York to Chicago. Two casual friends had been assigned adjoining seats. One was Jack, the other was the President of the University of Notre Dame. They renewed their acquaintance, and the two men talked of their vocation and what it meant in their lives. Jack spoke of his vision for change which he had begun to call "Ministry." It was meant to bring people of the church and others of good will together to better know each other. The President listened while Jack talked and began thinking of that portion of the University's facilities that were lying fallow under the summer sun. Before the plane landed they became partners to initiate this program of Ministry. Jack was invited to come to Notre Dame and lead the endeavor. Jack's heart skipped a beat. This was his chance to do so much for the Catholic church on a grand scale—for the poor, for the laity, and for the priesthood.

So Jack would go from an impoverished parish to large foundations where endowments were available for university buildings with new plumbing and twenty-year bonded roofs. Jack would carry out the endowment assignments asked of him by the President, and at the same time he would establish a Ministry program.

Soon the summer campus teemed. During those months, mothers would leave their household responsibilities and, for a time, return to the campus life of learning they loved. Diocesan priests would gather from across the nation to face their mutual problems, and dedicated missionaries would come from around the world. All people of good will were welcome. Many families made a week on campus their summer experience. It was Jack's dream come to life, and yet, there was something that *tugged*. He knew he belonged in his home diocese, a short ninety miles away.

A few years down the pike when the President of DePaul University in the heart of Chicago sought help to bring Christian Ministry into his school's curriculum, he asked Jack if he could be of help. A new cardinal, the fourth during Jack's priesthood, had recently been appointed to the Archdiocese. Things worked out well. Saying a fond farewell to his friends at Notre Dame, Jack returned home to take up residence at the rectory of Holy Name Cathedral.

He now works with the staff of DePaul University bringing Ministry to all races and creeds in Chicago's urban complex. During his long priestly career, neither bristles nor thorns have deterred this bantam rooster as he's worked to carry out his dreams. Jack knew his long-ago hero Pope John XXIII was ready and willing to accept resistance when he opened the window and planted the seed for change.

STAR OF INDIA

My son Paul said, "Dad, have you ever ridden in one of our Chicago taxis driven by a man from India?" He went on, "Just mention the name of Cyriac Kappil and that driver will tell how he, his family or his Indian neighbors were helped by Cyriac. Dad, You remember Cyriac!"

Cyriac Kappil (ka-<u>Pill</u>)—the name has a ring to it like a song or a poem.

It was a cold Easter morning in the early 1960s when we met. Cyriac was sixteen years old, neatly dressed in British-style clothes and he spoke with the preciseness of an English youth. He was, however, an Indian who had arrived by ship from the State of Kerala located at the southern tip of India. It took over thirteen thousand sea-going miles to reach New York. In India Cyriac had won a full scholarship to St. Mary's College in Winona, Minnesota, and he was on his way there.

His older sister, Mercy, a college friend of our daughter Carol, was spending the Easter holiday as our house guest. Cyriac called early Easter morning from a bus depot and Carol directed him to our front door. We found an extra bed for the young man and he stayed with us a couple of days until he could get on with his new life. Eager young students whose parents could offer them passage and a very limited stipend would come to the United States from around the world for their education.

That cold Easter afternoon, my wife Mary suggested things would work better for her if the two guests and three of our own children were taken for a ride. Mary would keep our other two children at home to help her prepare a feast of lamb. Taking a Sunday ride was a weekly occurrence. I had gathered a list of places to visit. That day's choice was an arboretum in Lincoln Park on the near north side of Chicago. It was a large building made of iron and glass filled with flowering trees, plants and, to celebrate Easter, a lavish display of lilies. Inside it was warm, moist and crowded. Outside it was cold and windy with wisps of snow. Ushers kept the crowd moving. Seeing the flowers was a delightful way to anticipate and welcome the coming of spring. Later when we returned home, Mary served a festive and delicious dinner: a large leg of lamb seasoned with garlic, vegetables, salad, and a dessert of light cake shaped like a lamb with shredded coconut for its coat of wool.

After Easter our brood returned to school. Carol and Mercy left for St. Mary's College at Notre Dame, Indiana, while Cyriac took his small valise and headed for the forests of Minnesota to attend St. Mary's College in Winona where he had won the four-year scholarship.

During his college years we saw Cyriac only when he visited Chicago maybe once a year or so. He would bring along his latest report card and it would always be topnotch. He was a tall, handsome, intelligent young man with a British accent and a rapid flow of words.

Cyriac wanted to become a lawyer and he talked about his plans to his parents in India. He wanted to be of help to others, particularly Indians living in Chicago. Having been graduated with honors from St. Mary's College, he returned to Chicago where he entered the college of law at Loyola University. Entering law school was expensive, and during one of his visits Cyriac was explaining to me about a money shortfall. He wasn't asking me for financial help because he had a principle of his own never to ask for or accept money from me. That's what made it easy for us to talk. What I didn't know was that before he left for home that day Mary had put an envelope in his overcoat pocket. In a few days Mary received a signed note with interest to be paid and an expiration date. That expiration date occurred during winter and it was bitter cold. Cyriac arrived at our front door nearly frozen. He had the total payment plus interest in cash. When Mary expressed concern that Cyriac might be frostbitten, we learned he had walked seven miles in order to make prompt payment. Needless to say, Mary made sure that he was warmed, fed, and taken home by car.

While at law school he took a full-time position as a sales representative for a pharmaceutical house and kept up his grades on very little sleep. (Cyriac's older sister, meanwhile, was pursuing a medical degree in Italy.)

Cyriac was very sociable, easy to talk to, and had an abiding curiosity about life. Once during the law school years he turned up at our house on a Sunday afternoon with a brand-new white car. He was so good at selling medical supplies to drug store owners that his employers had provided him with transportation so he could make more calls. He was now over six feet tall, spare as a rod. Did I tell you he was handsome? He sure was!

In time there came another graduation and Cyriac received his law degree from Loyola. A celebration was held at an Indian restaurant and our family was invited. Just thinking back about that food my tongue begins to burn and my mouth feels like it's on fire.

Cyriac passed the bar exam and started his own law firm. One Sunday he stopped by and told us he was returning to India. Family preparations had been made. When he arrived in India, Cyriac was invited to dinner at homes where there were marriageable daughters in residence. He visited with several fine families and made his choice. At no time was he ever alone with any of these young ladies. Cyriac and his bride were married in the Catholic Church and very shortly thereafter he left for the

United States alone. His wife Valsa arrived three months later and they moved into small quarters.

Cyriac asked if I could help Valsa find work, and thanks to good friends employment was found. She started as a social worker at Cook County Hospital. Valsa was a beautiful, petite, well educated Indian woman. She was soft-spoken and dressed in the finest Asian fashion. She earned many promotions leading to a highly responsible position at that large institution.

About this time, Cyriac was adding younger lawyers to his practice. He and Valsa had two children and moved to a suburban home with a large mortgage.

A year or so later Cyriac was pictured in the Chicago newspapers as the lawyer representing ex-Prime Minister of India, Margi DeSai in some controversy. Cyriac, in his capacity as counsel, had contacted Dr. Henry Kissinger, former United States Secretary of State, and Dr. Kissinger agreed to come to Chicago to testify.

Cyriac still stopped by on an occasional Sunday with Valsa and the children and always brought a gift from India for Mary. Cyriac and I had now been friends for some twenty years. More and more he became the spokesperson for the interests of his people. He loved cars and would gauge the progress he was making by the new or used car that he owned.

At this time one of his clients was a litigant in a procedure over money and property rights. Two brothers were haggling over the family estate. A deposition was ordered to be taken in Cyriac's law office. Cyriac represented one brother and another lawyer represented the other brother. A comely court reporter was present to take dictation. All was in readiness when the opposing brother asked to be excused for a moment to use the washroom. A few seconds later he reappeared with a gun. He killed his brother, killed Cyriac, and was pointing the gun at the court reporter when a young lawyer attacked from behind and forced him to the ground. The shot intended for the court reporter missed.

There was life the moment before—the moment after all the goodness, all the joy, all the fineness of character—all gone.

The city as well as its Indian community grieved for the loss of this fine young man. As my son Paul says, "Just ask any Indian you meet about Cyriac."

Cyriac Kappil—the name with a ring to it like a song or a poem.

The Glow of Embers

THE RESCUED RESCUER

He was driven. All through his life he was always reaching out to see what he could find. He was judgmental and loved to argue any and every point. It isn't a surprise he took up law. He was constantly competing—in sports, with his friends, with his relatives, with his wife, and to his detriment, with his children. A grownup shouldn't wrestle his son in earnest when it means eventual sure defeat for the son. It was brutal. It certainly couldn't be called fun. The son was turned away. It could be considered a form of child abuse—physically, and even more important, psychologically.

As for his background, he had an Irish father, Bill, a self-made success who was wont to say that anyone could do anything if he only tried hard enough. What this father most wanted was for his son to become a quarterback on the Notre Dame football team. To see the team he loved so much play a game, the father would drive his family 80-some miles each fall to the home games. On the way there, they would stop by the side of the road and have a picnic lunch. If it were cold or even cool, there would be a bottle of bourbon, and paper cups for all. When they were in grammar school, the bourbon would be mixed with soda pop or milk. The father drank straight from the bottle like it was water. (There were four children in the family. All in their turn became alcoholics.)

Kevin was the oldest son and very intelligent. He was also the one designated by the father to become a quarterback. He earned a law degree at Notre Dame and an advanced degree at Georgetown University in Washington. He went to Georgetown on a scholarship. No, he didn't get to quarterback at Notre Dame, or even get on the team. He wasn't quick enough at the game, just an *average Joe*. His father, Bill, thought he should have tried harder. As for his scholastic accomplishments, his father said anyone could do that.

So Kevin looked elsewhere for acceptance. During World War II, he was an FBI agent looking for spies here in the states. With his scholarship, his Irish smile, and ever-aggressive approach, he was ready for the world when the war ended. His FBI background was also an asset; its agents were promoted as elitists by J. Edgar Hoover.

It was around this time that Dick, my roommate, and I joined Kevin for a week's vacation. We had a fourth vacationer join us. He was Kevin's Uncle Jim, Bill's brother, and an alcoholic. We headed for northern Wisconsin where we would stay at the summer home of Kevin's family. On the ride up, when we stopped for gas or food, Uncle Jim would take off. Kevin would go and "find" him and bring him back to the car. We all knew where he was—in the nearest bar. It still took Kevin ten minutes or so to lead him back to our car, so we could continue our journey. The place we were heading for in northern Wisconsin was about a seven-hour drive from Chicago, so we made a few stops along the road, and each time it was the same. Uncle Jim took off, and Kevin brought him back. One night while we were staying at the summer home, Uncle Jim took off for town. Kevin went to get him. They got back about 2 a.m. from a town three miles away. Someone smarter might have guessed that my roommate Dick and I were on vacation with two drunks.

Later when he joined the business world, Kevin, with his winning Irish smile, gained ready acceptance. He was the bakery owners' representative in their labor relations contracts with the

Baker's Union. Each was a major entity—owners and unions slugged out their differences; Kevin had learned from his father to be a ruthless fighter.

As Kevin rose in importance, his image of himself couldn't keep up with the pace. His own success, as he saw it, was nothing compared to that of others. The homes of others were bigger, their cars more expensive, their club memberships a deliberate affront to him. And so he was overtaken by the Irish curse—drink and forget, drink and relax, drink and you'll like yourself—with *drink and be damned* the outcome. So much talent lost to so much self-shame.

He had become estranged from his wife, his family, and his few friends. All he had was his drive to stay alive. He finally sought help. He tried and he failed, and he tried again—how many times I'll never know—but a few years down the road he won. He won in time to see and care for his wife during her last illness. (She was dying from Lou Gehrig's disease.) He worked to recover a lost friendship with his children.

Kevin had fathered four children, Kevin Jr., Herman, Helen, and Billie. Kevin Jr. is a successful business man with a lovely wife and a fine family. Herman is a college professor in Wisconsin, and a great outdoors man. Helen, Kevin's only daughter, has had a tough life. Unfortunately, she fell two stories in a bizarre accident when she was three. When it happened, Kevin came from the hospital to tell us about it, and to take a tumbler of whisky and down it in one gulp. Billie, the youngest, and an aspiring actor, had one stint on Broadway—a play with a cast of four. Billy played one of two sons. The leads were played by an accomplished actor and actress. The story wasn't well received by the critics, and the play closed in two weeks. Alcohol wasn't a problem for Kevin's wife or for any of his children.

Now Kevin's drive was as strong as ever, but it was directed toward saving others. In downtown Chicago, there was a restaurant called Toffinetti's with a long counter on one side. The end of that counter was for men or women in trouble, good people who knew that without help they were going to fall again, and that one drink would turn into a hundred. Kevin was a regular at the counter, sitting there with the everlasting cup of coffee and waiting for someone who might need help. They listened to him, he'd been there.

Alcoholics Anonymous began to place great trust in him. When he could get time off from his job with a law firm, he would fly to Vegas to rescue someone. The list of important people he brought home is impressive. He is still doing this today. Some people reading this might well remember the day Kevin came into their own lives on a rescue mission. He never looks back, he just hopes to find strength and self-worth from his work of rescuing others.

MICHAEL

One of the saddest young men and the young man who came closest to breaking my heart was Michael. He was a good person, used, abused, and victimized; and it all began when he was very young.

He was the sixth child in a family of eight, living near the side of a mountain in Iran. His town was small, and his family was poor. Michael had a gift for mathematics; he seemed to grasp principles without having to be taught. Before he was twelve, he was an advanced mathematician.

One day, his family was visited by an agent of a large oil interest in Saudi Arabia. This man had heard of the boy's talent and wished to have him work in the oil fields. The boy's parents listened to what the agent had to say. Soon a contract was signed that would bring the family out of poverty. It was a five-year contract, during which time the family would be sent eighty percent of Michael's earnings each month. The oil company's agent took Michael away to Saudi Arabia—away from his family, away from his home, away from his friends. His family began receiving the bulk of Michael's earnings, and they no longer knew poverty.

When Michael arrived at the work site, he learned he would be over 100 miles into the desert amid pipes, oil rigs, metal huts, and men. The 12-year-old boy became part of a team of 38 men who lived and worked in the desert monitoring the flow of oil to the outside world. Every two weeks, a helicopter would hover over the outpost to drop mail and provisions, and pick up a package of outgoing mail. In a few minutes it would be gone, leaving some of the amenities of life behind—like good food and movies.

Desert sand ranged on all sides of the landscape interrupted only by the big pipes pumping oil to the outside world. Every night Michael regretted having the talent that had brought about this separation from his family. Each night he cried himself to sleep. There were no other boys on the site he could relate to; there were just 38 men and Michael.

On occasion, important representatives from the American company providing the expertise to the Saudis would arrive and spend a few days at the installation. One of these men, an executive of the American company, made a number of visits. When Michael was a handsome young man of nearly 16, that representative made arrangements for him to be transferred to the company's home office in New York. En route, Michael would be given time to return home and renew his family relationships.

So Michael went home four years after he had left, and he felt alienated. He didn't quite know how to act with his family—his world had become so different. The family was Catholic, but Michael had forsaken his faith and was ridden with guilt.

Michael was flown to New York, and four years later the corporate executive and Michael were transferred to Chicago. When I met Michael, he was twenty years old. He was still providing a good living for his parents, brothers and sisters. The oil company representative had taken residence in grand style only a few blocks from my home in Chicago. I never met him.

When I first met Michael, he was a small, very quiet young man who had a sad smile and a most imaginative manner. He seemed haunted by his early Catholicism. A younger brother came to the states shortly after, and the two of them shared an apartment on Chicago's north side.

Michael was the corporate executive's plaything. The executive, by dint of psychological control, could make him eat meat on Friday, avoid Mass on Sunday, or have Michael do whatever he demanded. Michael seemed helpless to separate himself from the relationship. When Michael was away from this influence, however, he seemed to be a most kindly 24-year-old adult. He had a well-paying job and, in time, would bring his mother to this country. In Iran, his father had good employment as a chauffeur at the American Embassy. Michael's family was doing well.

Maybe some do-good organization or person brought Michael and me together. He was looking for a friend, and at the time I was learning how to listen. I remember Michael coming to our house with a whole cabload of presents when he was invited to Christmas dinner. His present to me was my first electric razor.

I would see him maybe once a month for lunch or when he'd come to dinner with the family. He wasn't great at talking but was eager to please, and found comfort being in our home. It was the only real home he had been in since he was a boy of twelve. One night after dinner, I offered to drive him home. We left at eight, and it was a short drive. When I got home, it was eleven o'clock. In the dark, sitting in the car, this boy who had supported his family through the years so generously poured out the story of his terrible life and the troubled person he was.

Michael continued trying to make peace with himself, and with God through the church. A priest had suggested that he unburden himself to a friend or someone he could trust. Since Michael had no friends, he asked if I would listen and if maybe I could help him. I said I would try. I think being at the dinner table with a family helped him to speak out about his background. He had been taken from the security of his home while so young, and had grown up a used person—first by the men in the camp, and then by his sponsor. This boy-man cried; he was in deep shame and, as I was to learn, he had little will left to make any change in his life. He was earning a fine salary for his math talents and he was still sending most of it home to his parents in

Iran. I did the only thing I was able to do, I was a friend and listened as he told me about the lonesomeness in his life.

A few months later, I received a call from Michael's brother who asked if he could put his mother on the phone. She had come to this country to visit her sons. She was crying, and her English was poor. I didn't understand, but I said I'd come to their apartment. The brother now lived in the apartment adjacent to Michael's with their mother. When I got there, the brother told me that he was joining the United states Navy to get away from Michael who he feared was going to kill him. The mother said Michael no longer worked, and that she too was afraid for herself. They had called Iran and, with the help of the Ambassador's staff, Michael's father was given a visa to come to the States.

Since Michael had locked himself inside his apartment, I suggested they do likewise and wait for the husband and father to arrive from Iran. I assured them that I had no intention of trying to make contact with Michael or the knife and gun he had been brandishing. I told them to keep their door locked and wait, asking them to call me if I could be of help.

A day or so later, a man speaking excellent English informed me over the phone that he was Michael's father. He asked if we could meet and talk. I picked him up and we parked out by the Adler Planetarium along the shore of Lake Michigan. He knew all about my family, and how much his son loved us; and told me how grateful he and his wife were. He then asked me if there was anything I knew that might have caused Michael to "go mad."

I began slowly talking of Michael's horrendous sense of guilt, a guilt he seemed unable to resolve and had great difficulty talking about. What help Michael sought hadn't been equal to the problem. He had recently told me, however, that he was feeling better about himself. The father asked whether there was anything else I could tell him. So I finally told him what I knew about the man in Michael's life, and hoped the father would not go seeking revenge. Michael's father told me he would leave punishment to

God. He seemed to know better than I did what had happened to his son. He thanked me and said he'd be in touch.

A week later, Michael's father phoned to say that things had not improved, and that he had asked government people for help. It had been recommended that, for his own safety, Michael should be institutionalized. His parents had received the necessary papers and signed them, and the commitment papers had been served. Could I help them get Michael there? Police would be present to see that the transfer was carried out safely.

The father said, "I think if you come, Michael will go peacefully." So I went, and Michael, who still had just enough contact with reality to know me, docilely held my hand and followed me.

The police remained out of sight in the background. At the Illinois State Psychiatric Institution, they welcomed Michael in a friendly manner, and then let him know he was in their charge. Since Michael couldn't weep for himself, I think I did. His parents were deeply moved.

During the following weeks, Michael's father and mother flew home to Iran. The father couldn't afford to jeopardize his job. Michael's brother joined the Navy and was shipped off to training camp. Time passed, and I wondered about Michael. Not being a relative, I was told by the authorities that I would have limited access to information, and no visiting rights. So Michael and I were cut off from each other for all practical purposes.

One night two years later, I received a phone call. It was Michael. It was a different Michael who was slow to speak with a halting voice. He told me he was out on his own and had a job. I was pleased.

I said, "Michael, could we get together?" He didn't answer. Finally I said, "Are you there Michael?" The silence continued, and I waited. When he spoke, Michael said he didn't think so. There was a pause. I waited. Michael then said his past was gone, was over—buried. The doctor said he could call me this once but that was all. He then asked me not to try and find him. He was trying to make a go of it holding on to the present. Another moment's pause, and he addressed me in his native Aryan or Zend tongue. It was a phrase we often exchanged on meeting or leaving each other. It meant "My good friend." A moment later, the phone went dead. Michael had hung up.

I know nothing more. I wanted to, but I didn't try to find him, and I never heard from his family. I miss him.

STINGRAY

His first name was Raymond, but he preferred to be called Ray. It was apt. He could sting like the fish. He liked doing it. When he was a small boy growing up, he was often stung by adults—it hurt. Now he had power to do the stinging. It all depends on power—if you've got it you can sting, if you don't you get stung. His whole name was Raymond D. Kendall, and when I met him he headed the purchasing department for construction at International Harvester Company.

It was at a time when Harvester was a great company, with sales all over the world; and the founder's name, McCormick, stood for donations to the city's libraries and opera houses, as well as the Art Institute and all sorts of city projects. The International Harvester Company no longer exists as such, taken down by bad management and over-aggressive union tactics. It was a time when management and labor fought bare-knuckled, and in the end neither won. During that time people got hurt, some got killed. Often it takes all-out war to prepare the way for a more sensible approach. Sometimes everything goes down.

Raymond Kendall held his position at a time when International Harvester was in full flower as a leading manufacturer of farm equipment and the producer of more heavy-duty trucks than any other manufacturer. These were just two of a myriad of products the company made and sold. And so, Ray was flying high—salary raises and large, yearly bonuses. It hadn't always been like that.

Ray grew up in the midwest. His father, Frank, was addicted to pool halls and gambling spots, not that he had the money for such but that was where he spent his time. Frank was a hanger-on, an odd-job temporary employee with one goal in mind—money. To get what he needed he was adept at borrowing. There are people in small midwest towns who still hold some of his IOUs. He was forever on the go and it wasn't friends he left behind.

Frank was married to Rose, and Ray was their only child. Rose loved her roué husband so much she couldn't leave him. Over and over again, Frank would wear out his welcome in a town, and depart (mostly at night), destination unknown, leaving Rose and little Raymond without money or food, staggering under the debts Frank had accumulated. In order for mother and son to survive, Ray learned how to steal just to have basic food and clothing. After Frank's departure, mother and son would somehow survive until Frank surreptitiously got in touch. Then at night, Rose and her son Ray would leave town, catch up with Frank, and start the next chapter in their "life with father."

Ray couldn't tell you how many grammar schools he attended, but he could remember the number of high schools—it was eleven. Name a small town in Indiana, Illinois or Iowa, and he could tell you the name of the school. Ray was small—only five feet, four inches—so as a new boy at school he knew what to expect. Ray didn't fight fair, he just fought to win. Big fellows were left hunkered, crunched over, unable to walk. During those years, he didn't remember ever having a friend. Maybe by then he didn't know how to be one either.

Young Ray's father died in a fight, and Rose slowly lost contact with her son and the rest of the world. She eventually passed away in the public ward of a hospital. When she died, Ray was old enough to be a high school graduate, but he wasn't. He had never had an opportunity to show anyone he was smart. He was all alone, and to survive he took a job at International Harvester. He began a career that flourished. He was attentive, resourceful, and at last he was able to stay in one location. No more running. The plant where he worked had a baseball team, and Ray became the second baseman. For the first time in his life, Ray heard people cheer for him. He had found in Harvester a place where he could belong. They even helped him with his education, and in time he earned a high school diploma. The plant continued to promote him. He was going places, and he found a bride to join him—Joyce. She was as docile and devoted to him as his mother had been to her Frank.

Climbing the corporate ladder is rough. Just ask anyone caught up in it. You've no time to look behind you—just time to keep fighting for what is yours. Even the executive washroom key can become an important credential.

Ray and Joyce had two lovely daughters who grew up, went to college, and later married. It was about this time that I came into his life or, rather, that Ray came into mine. It began as a business relationship. I was selling roof replacements to large industries, and he was the buyer for such products at Harvester. My father, as president of the family business, introduced us, and Ray and I got to know each other. Later, I succeeded to my father's position, and the business relationship with Ray and Harvester went on for many years. Though never mentioned or alluded to, he seemed to treat me as a son.

Ray was never able to forget where he came from or that he was a jungle fighter in a corporate world. He often mentioned that he'd never had a friend, and that included me since he was certain I was only around for business reasons. The people he associated and socialized with were, without exception, like me—salesmen seeking contracts from the mighty corporation—and Ray was the one who held the keys to our success. He was the one who had the contracts to give.

Every Friday, I would pick him up at corporate headquarters and we would drive a few blocks to a private club. We would have a couple of cocktails, lunch, and relentless, ceaseless gin rummy. I didn't let him win, he just did. The money we bet was reasonable. He could beat the pants off me and I'm not that bad at the game. He never forgot a single card that had been turned up. Late in the game he would know what was still in the pack. On some rare occasions, he would show up and we would talk. He did the talking, and over and over I would hear about all the rascals he had to deal with. He had enemies galore.

Twice during these years, the company's internal auditing division informed Ray that they were planning an audit of his office to be scheduled at his convenience sometime within the following week. His response to the auditors was to put on his hat and coat and give them the keys to his office. Ray would take an impromptu vacation until the auditors were through. That way, he said, they could be sure he didn't move or destroy anything or tamper with evidence of possible wrongdoing. Throughout the corporation, all departments were systematically audited and it was no big thing. Ray, however, considered it a personal attack, a question of his integrity and part of a plot to destroy him. He sure could bristle.

Late one night I was driving Ray to his suburban home after a poker game attended by the five other salesmen and myself. Outside it was cold and dark, in the car it was warm and quiet. That night he had won at poker (as usual), and was in good spirits (for Ray). It was while driving him home after poker games that I learned all I knew about how he'd grown up. On this one occasion, in the dark of the car, he seemed for a moment vulnerable to his feelings of being alone—but only for a moment. When I told him I would like him to consider me a friend, he scoffed. Then I told him he meant more to me than the Harvester account and that I would be glad to prove it. He became quiet. He stayed quiet. Maybe I'd gone too far, I sure didn't want to lose my best account. I kept waiting. What was he thinking? When he finally spoke, I could hardly hear him. He said, "If you want to think that you are my friend, I can't stop you." Nothing more, just that.

The year his boss retired, Ray thought of himself as one of three men to be considered for the promotion. He was never called, he was never interviewed, and he would never speak to the man who got the promotion—his new boss. It wasn't long before he was offered the chance for an early retirement. It wasn't a chance, it was a choice—either take it or be terminated. Ray had been with International Harvester for 42 years. He only knew how to fight, not fairly, but to win. Ray finally lost.

On his last day at the office, he went around saying goodbye to those who had worked under him—about a dozen people. In their time and in various ways, they'd all been hurt or put down by him. To each of those people he said he'd thought he'd been more than fair in his dealings. Before the person could reply, he said he would like to sit down for a last word that afternoon, and he went around the office setting an appointed time when he would meet with each of these employees.

That same day, when I phoned my office about 11 a.m., there was a message to forget whatever I was doing and meet Ray for lunch at a downtown hotel. The group of five poker-playing salespeople, who like myself sold services to Harvester, sat around the table. The reason for the get-together was to let us know that he had set up the afternoon's "goodbye meetings." He had a pretty good idea what he would hear, and he knew it wouldn't be pleasant. So from the start, he had no intention of going back—ever. When he told us, we joined with him giving hollow, hapless laughs. His early lessons about life hadn't changed—it was a war.

Ray retired to Florida where he built a home. I wrote him, and I called him. Joyce would answer, and say he was out. He was always out. He was so good to me for so many years, I had hoped that he would let me be his friend. I'll never know. A couple of years later, I learned that he had died in a motel room, all alone.

The Glow of Embers

LORDY

Lucille was her name. She was married to Leo. Their last name was Lord. They had a small son named Peter. Peter was destined to be the last pope. Lucille was the one who told us. She was the one in contact.

The Lords had a meager life, what with Leo being an assistant janitor at various parishes. Leo also took up Sunday collections at the direction and supervision of the pastor, wearing his good suit. There was one occasion when he wore his suit to act as best man at a wedding. It was an evening affair—two young people showed up at the rectory and, based on information they had received that day, insisted they be married. So, Leo was called to be best man, or witness. The marriage would be a surprise to the parents of the young couple.

Lucille, meanwhile, mostly waited for angels (she once told me they really have wings) or for an occasional long-gone saint to visit her bearing messages. That's how she knew little Peter's destiny. The Lords had a small coterie of people who lived this exciting life with them, participating in small evening meetings. For the Lords, the future looked good, if not the present.

It happened during a period when Leo had time on his hands. He created a statue at Lucille's suggestion. He used old iron and clothes hangers as the basic structure in his design. The statue was to be of Christ. Plaster was the medium he used to cover the metal framing. All in all, when he finished, it wasn't too bad an effort. Hands are always hard to form—and this Christ wore a lot of clothes which might have covered other shortcomings as well. In the hollow that existed inside the form, Leo placed a small electric motor, and he also used a borrowed piece of rubber as the statue's chest. This was to be a statue of the Throbbing Heart. When it was ready to be shown, you could place your head against the statue's breast and sure enough you could feel and hear the Throbbing Heart—if the motor was turned on.

Lucille kept waiting for Rome to respond to her voluminous correspondence. She was writing, at the direction of her spiritual friends, to about a dozen prelates. While she received no answer through the mail, she did know about things happening in Rome. *Things* meant another holy day to be established, dedicated to Christ's Throbbing Heart, as witnessed through Leo's statue.

A while ago I wrote about Bunny, a Marine pilot killed in the second World War. Well, at the time of this statue, Bunny was in Chicago expecting word from the Marines. He had asked me if there was some temporary work he could do as he awaited the call. He knew I led a construction company that often put trucks on the road carrying material and equipment to out-of-town job sites. Driving a truck out of town and back would suit Bunny just fine. Well, there was a truck being loaded for a trip to Louisville, Kentucky, and I hired Bunny to drive it. A little while later I received a phone call—it was Lucille. She told me that she, Leo, and the someday-to-be "last pope" had been directed by her contact friends to leave Chicago and take up residence near Gethsemane Seminary, which is close to Louisville, Kentucky. They were ready to leave, having few personal effects to take with them, but did not know what to do with the statue. So, Lucille's call was to ask me if I could help her—just as a truck was being loaded that Bunny would drive to our Louisville job site. (What would cynics say to that!)

Bunny was directed to stop at the Lord's basement apartment and pick up the statue and Leo, who would accompany it on the truck ride. It was a cold and wet trip and the highways were two-lane and bumpy. The truck arrived the next day and delivered the material and equipment to the job site. It then proceeded to the new abode of the Lord family close to the seminary.

Bunny and Leo climbed up onto the bed of the truck to remove the statue. It wasn't there, but then again—it was. The Throbbing Heart statue had lost its plaster during the rough truck ride, and what they found were small pieces of plaster lying at the bottom of the container in which the statue was packed. Only the motor and the rubber mat were still on the metal frame.

I was at the office late in the morning when Bunny called to tell me what happened. He also told of Leo's deep remorse. When Leo called Lucille to tell her what happened, she said that this was a sign that Leo should build a bigger statue. Then Bunny asked if there was anything I wanted him to do before returning to Chicago.

I thought for a moment and said, "No, I don't think so." Then, on second thought I said, "Bring me a relic!"

The Glow of Embers

A World Apart

The Glow of Embers

A World Apart

Fifty years ago, all across the country the federal government replaced the squalid, rat-infested, wooden fire traps where the poor lived with new, sanitary, fire-resistant 19-story dwellings. Today the buildings are being blasted to the ground; it is the end of an unsuccessful experiment. The following sketches describe life in one of the projects, the Robert Taylor Homes in Chicago.

The Glow of Embers

OUR BEGINNING

It began as a summer program in 1963. The Illinois Department of Public Aid told me that there were thousands of young men in the public housing projects, none of whom had a male adult in his life. At the time I was looking for a way to be of help to others. (So much had come my way—a good home, a fine education, a lovely wife, healthy children, and a successful business career.) The department offered to provide a social worker on "released time" to assist me. Her name was Winnie Freeman, a charming black woman. The boys came to love this warm and gracious person. So did I.

A local Jesuit high school offered me the use of a school bus and we were soon in business. I called Winnie to see if she could help on Wednesday afternoons, and she could. A notice was sent out to welfare mothers announcing that a new program was available for young men which would provide an opportunity for them to see the city. There were twelve young men between the ages of 11 and 17 at our first meeting and we had lots to do and much to talk about. The number of boys in the group soon rose to thirty-five. They elected (we voted on everything) to name their club "Cultural Enrichment for Boys." I think their school teachers must have contributed to a name with such long words in it.

All of the boys in the Club lived in the Robert Taylor Homes, a public housing project (still one of the largest of its kind in the world), standing along a mile of State Street in Chicago. These boys were without fathers in their lives.

The breakdown of the family often came about like this: the husband worked for Wisconsin Steel. The newspaper said Wisconsin Steel was cutting back by 1500 jobs. The husband was one of the 1500 let go. The husband and his wife were barely getting by. Within a week, there would be no food for their children, so the mother applied to a government agency for help. She learned it was easier and quicker to qualify for food, lodging and maintenance money if she was abandoned, alone and desperate. Believe me, that's how it worked. So the good father left his family (it's called "desertion"), and went searching for another job.

When the mother and her children were moved into the project, they were instructed by the social worker that "deserting" husbands were neither permitted to live in, or visit the quarters supplied by the government. The lonesome husbands (and fathers) would visit their families at the project anyway. When that happened, the children of such families had a dozen ways of warning their parents of the presence of the social worker on the site. Both husband and wife were grateful for this arrangement.

For the most part, these boys lived their lives at the project. About half of them had never seen Lake Michigan, one of the world's greatest lakes, less than a mile from where they lived. Besides going to school, their education about life was learned in the open area between high-rises. It was quite a liberal education based on the art of how to use people, and how to avoid being used.

When the White Sox played in nearby Comiskey Park, the young men in the project could see the lights and they could hear the fireworks go off when the Sox hit a homer; yet none of the boys had ever been to the ballpark. So we went.

A magnificent world was ours to discover, with me at the wheel of the borrowed school bus. Food of one kind or another was a part of our trips. When we visited a large bakery and the boys had stuffed themselves, each was given a bag of food to take home. Wherever we went we found Chicago to be a generous city.

On one of the last of our summer trips that year, before the boys returned to school, we went to a steel mill, and afterwards we stopped at my home and had hamburgers in the backyard. The boys were impressed. My neighbors, as I was soon to hear, were less so. (Integration was still in the future.)

On our return to the Robert Taylor Homes, a group of the boys asked me if they could do something to continue their Club. Especially, they said, they would miss having someone to talk to. Who could say no?

I talked with Winnie and we decided to meet with the boys on Wednesday afternoons after school at the project, and on Saturday mornings at my home.

During the school year, Wednesday meetings were concerned with education. Report cards were important so that those with problems could be helped. If a boy's arithmetic was poor, another member who did well in math was assigned to help him. Everyone had to stand up and give a talk. The Club had spelling contests. There were prizes for good performances, and Winnie decided who won. They found she wasn't to be fooled with—she meant business.

Winnie encouraged the boys to read newspapers and she would quiz them each week on what they read. The best reports were rewarded. Soon we were hearing recitations on subjects of national interest. The boys even went to the local library so they could read newspapers for free. We were encouraging them to be competitive in order to get ahead, rather than being passive, as they were in project life.

On Saturdays when we met at my home, carfare to and from was provided. Our formal meetings, with Club officials in charge and big decisions to discuss, were held in the living room.

I remember one particular exercise we worked on with the boys which had to do with a *New Yorker* magazine advertisement and a tape recorder. Winnie and I would work with one boy at a time in a small ante room. He would read an ad, and if there were words he didn't know, we would help with comprehension or pronunciation. When the young man was ready, the tape recorder would be turned on, and he would recite the ad. After his first recitation, we would work to refine his diction. We would ask him to speak more distinctly, and to pronounce every syllable, with particular attention to word endings. The boy would be given some time alone so that he could repeat the process with the tape recorder running. At the end of an hour or so, one of us would come in and run the tape back to the boy's first attempt, and then ahead to his last.

I remember one of the members saying about his last recitation, "Boy, I sounded just like I was on the radio!"

This was in sharp contrast to "project talk," their first language, which Winnie kept insisting they must change if they wished to join the world outside.

As a reward when free time had been earned, recreational activities were made available in the basement where there was a pool table and a ping pong area. I sculpted in clay, and so did the boys. Each week we voted on whose burgers and soft drinks we would bag in for lunch. If we made a mess, Winnie saw to it that the house was in apple-pie order before the boys left.

That's how Cultural Enrichment for Boys came into being. The Club could have included girls from the start, but that's the way it was thirty years ago. The group did include girls during its time, so we weren't the last to lay the old aside. For those who wanted to, the Club offered a way to see and know the world outside the project, and the potential some day, hopefully, to be able to live there.

A ROLY-POLY NEW MEMBER

John Taylor was one of the youngest boys in the Club. He was also roly-poly, and the last picked when games were played and sides were chosen. He wasn't shy, however. He had an opinion on every issue and a great curiosity about life. He was also courteous, with a great respect for my wife and daughters. A few years later, when the Club dissolved, John didn't accept it. He was eleven or twelve then. He used the phone to keep in contact.

Today, John is in his mid-thirties, he's six-feet-two, and close to 200 pounds. He lives in California where he monitors blood during operations at a large hospital. He has traveled to Europe as a soloist for a singing group. He has been a big brother to many young men, and he gives of himself to people who are poor, or in trouble. He is very proud of his son, a musician and high school student.

And John has never forgotten the Club, or its top dog. Through all the intervening years, he has kept in close contact. He is certainly my good friend, and a son of mine who's always asked if he could call me Dad.

Some time ago John wrote the following story telling how he joined the Club, which came about because food was paramount in project life and, like animals, the boys always seemed to be foraging.

One morning my brother Ronny came shaking me awake saying my friend Renard was at the door. I slid from the bottom bunk of our sheet metal bunk beds and said:

"What he want?"

"I don't know," Ronny replied.

I grabbed my jeans, gym shoes, and T-shirt and headed to the bathroom to wipe my drool-stained face.

"Tell him to come on in."

Renard came to the bathroom door grinning like he found some food stamps.

"Geechi, I want you to go somewhere wit' me."

"Where?"

"4844, there's this lady giving away food and stuff."

"What you mean givin' it away, what you gotta do for it?"

"Nothin', just listen to her talk about stuff."

"What stuff?"

"Just come on wit' me, she make some good sandwiches."

"Alright."

Renard and I ran downstairs across the big central playground and over to 4844. We went to #102 and Renard knocked on the screen door. The door opened and there stood this lady looking at us and smiling.

"Hi, Miss Freeman. This my friend Geechi. Can he come in?"

"Why yes, but what did you say your name was?"

"Geechi."

"Never heard of anyone named that before. Who named you?"

"My daddy."

"So Daddy named you. Why Geechi? It's so unusual."

"Cause that's what we are."

"Geechies?"

"Yes ma'am."

"Well, nice to meet you Geechi. Come on in."

This place wasn't arranged like an apartment, but more like an office. Miss Freeman was a small, slight, dark-skinned woman with a big, toothy, warm smile. There were long office tables with plastic table covers and eight chairs at each place. In front of each seat was a place setting: a little fork, a big fork, a knife, two spoons, and a paper napkin. It was nice, but why anybody would need so many forks and spoons beat me. The kitchen was spotless; everything looked new. There was a washing machine and dryer too, and I wondered whose clothes was she washing since nobody lived there.

Renard went in the bathroom. I could hear him washing his hands. He came out drying his hands, walked over to the kitchen cabinet and pulled out an apron.

"What you doin' with that on?" I asked Renard standing there with *Home Sweet Home* sewn across the top of his apron.

"I'm gettin' ready for the class."

"What class?" I asked.

"Just go wash your hands and come wit' me."

I went into the bathroom and was washing my hands thinking, "I didn't come here to put on no sissy apron or go to class! I want me some sandwiches. Doggone, Renard!"

Drying my hands, I went to the kitchen and Renard handed me an apron with a picture of *Pebbles* from the *Flintstones* on it.

"I don't like this, and where is my sandwiches?" I said.

Just then Miss Freeman came out of the back smiling. "Don't ya'll look cute!" I didn't like that either.

"Geechi, turn around, let me tie your apron." said Miss Freeman.

"What's the matter, Geechi?"

"Why come we gotta wear these sissy aprons? Renard said you was givin' out sandwiches."

"Well, they have to be made first, don't they?"

"I guess."

"Okay, well come on, we're going to make meat loaf sandwiches."

She said the magic word, *meat loaf*. There was a knock at the screen door and soon there were five other boys all in aprons organizing this lunch. It was fun and I eventually got over the apron.

Everybody had a job to do, mine was preparing the meat loaf with Renard and Miss Freeman. I'd never done the communal activity thing before, but it wasn't so bad except for the aprons. As we buzzed around the kitchen, Miss Freeman told us what this program was all about. She said there was a gentleman who was interested in helping project kids through "cultural enrichment," whatever that was. She said he would drop in from time to time to meet the kids, take them on field trips, and to his home sometimes.

Well, soon the place smelled like my mama's kitchen on Sunday evening. Everybody took off their aprons, washed their hands and moved to the tables. Miss Freeman and Renard served our meals as we sat.

"Now boys, take your napkins and place them over your right thigh."

Now this didn't make any sense to me.

I wondered, "Why come you cover up only one leg? What if the food all falls on the other leg?" I didn't get it but I did it anyway.

"Who would like to say the blessing?" asked Miss Freeman.

We looked around at each other and then Renard said, "I'll say it!"

"Over the teeth and under the gums watch out stomach, here it comes. Amen."

"Renard! Please, that isn't funny."

"Jesus wept," said Miss Freeman.

"Moses slept," mumbled Renard under his breath.

"Alright, let's start off with the salad," said Miss Freeman, just as some of us were stabbing our meat loaf, "fixin'" to make a sandwich.

"Now, no elbows on the table please."

"Your salad fork is the smaller one; use it first please."

"Why there's so many rules just to eat?" I asked.

"Geechi, these rules are referred to as etiquette. They're rules for dining."

"Well, why we only cover one leg with the napkin, what about the other one?"

"Geechi, I didn't write the rules, I just teach them. Now enjoy your meal."

Man, them was some good sandwiches or "sarniches" as they called them back then. All of us were as happy as we could be until Miss Freeman put down her fork and said:

"Stop! All of you. Put your sandwiches down."

Everybody looked up wondering what was wrong.

Miss Freeman said, "Please, can't you hear yourselves? It sounds like we're frying chicken, you all are smackin' so loud. Close your mouths when you chew!"

Wow! You would have thought you were in church, it got so quiet. She looked at us sitting there, lips all shiny, looking like she took our favorite toy. Then she burst out laughing. So did we.

"Now go on and eat, the food isn't going anywhere, so slow down."

"Yes ma'am," we said.

We had ice cream and pound cake for desert. Everybody was feeling good.

"Alright fellas, it's clean-up time."

"Clean up? We got to clean up too? Aw man," I said to Renard.

Renard said, "Geechi, this is the best part, wait and see."

"Okay," I said.

One after another, the other boys slipped out leaving me, Renard, Miss Freeman and the dishes. We knocked the dishes out and reset the tables.

"You boys were a big help today, thank you so much."

"Well looka here!" she said opening the oven door.

"I've got half a meat loaf left."

Renard nudged me and winked, "See I told you to wait," he whispered.

"This goes to my special helpers!"

Bingo! More "sarniches." Renard and I walked home with three sandwiches apiece smackin' all the way across the playground. Miss Freeman was nice and told me to come back again. I was an official member of the "Cronin Club"—whoever he was.

The Glow of Embers

A DIFFERENT KIND OF WAKE

He was a 300-pound black policeman out of uniform, but when you looked at the size of his shoes you just knew he was a cop. His real job was public relations officer at a large city high school. He had a club or night stick tied to his belt, which he said helped him at times to carry out his public relations. He was doing a favor for some friends of mine who thought I shouldn't be left on my own.

It was a hot summer night, and together this new friend and I drove to the Robert Taylor Homes located along State Street in downtown Chicago. This project is one of the largest in the world. We were going there to attend the wake of a young woman—used, abused, and discarded. Neither of us knew her. She was, however, the sister of Toby—one of the members of Cultural Enrichment for Boys, the group that met at my home each week and traveled the city together discovering a wider world.

When we arrived at the project, the open area between buildings was crowded with people. It was cooler to be outside the hulking high-rises than to be in them. We headed for the elevators of one in the buildings. Arriving, we waited in line as people were disgorged from the iron cages. Everyone was hot. When our turn came, it was a slow ride to the twelfth floor, our destination. Whenever people got off, others would get on, taking the ride up in order to be on for the ride down. Those wire cages stayed full.

Arriving at the twelfth floor, we got off and faced a fenced corridor which was open to the weather and ran across the south length of the building on each floor. The corridor was filled with people standing single-file up to the door of the apartment where the wake was being held. They were mostly women, dressed in their best on this hot night. Most of the people on welfare paid some small change each week from their monthly government stipend to buy a burial plan for their family. The plan included a half-hour showing of the deceased at the funeral parlor before burial. So waking was held at home.

We stood at the end of the line. I was glad I had on a coat to show proper respect. Soon I could see we were drawing attention, as people looked back at one big black man and the only white man in the neighborhood. In a little while a woman came back to us as a spokesperson. She asked us to accompany her to the front of the line. Since I heard no one object as we moved forward, it must have been through mutual agreement.

Again we waited outside the apartment. The noise from the people in the open court twelve floors below rose loud and raucous. No one was getting cooler. Shortly we were invited to go in, and I was introduced haltingly by my young friend, Toby, to his mother. Toby's eyes went out of his head at the sight of my friend. His mother invited us to partake of the food which was in abundant supply. The policeman and I met family members, said what you usually say on such occasions, and shortly left.

While walking back down the corridor, we noticed that each of the waiting women carried a food package; if the bereaved had plenty of food, she could sell her food stamps at a discount, and use the money for other kinds of purchases.

We waited again at the elevator to take our ride up in order to get down. At ground level, the curiosity of a white man on their turf at night had attracted a group of forty or so people.

News travels fast at the project. They even knew why we were there.

As we walked away, we could hear what they were saying. It was the same response they gave at church when they agreed with the preacher. They were saying, "Amen, amen."

The Glow of Embers

ANOTHER KIND OF ZOO

It was a Wednesday afternoon in the summertime—a time to spend with about 25 boys from the Robert Taylor Homes. It was our second year together.

We were going to the zoo. We'd been to a steel mill, a major league ball game, and to businesses that employed blacks. Along with the fun and food on these trips, there was a message, I hoped. Most times it came from an employee talking to the boys about the education and skills they needed in order to get a job.

The bus was waiting when I arrived at the high school, and in a few minutes I drove it to the Robert Taylor Homes. When I got there, the boys in the Club were waiting at a parking area, as agreed.

They began to load onto the bus. I knew most of the boys well; however, on occasion, some would bring friends who I would then meet for the first time. The last boy in the line was a new one. He didn't quite get into the bus—he got in just far enough to grab a hasp and pull the door shut. Then with a metal coat hanger, he sealed the door from the outside.

Realizing something was afoot, I started the bus and tried to move. Too late, rocks had been placed under a back wheel and the bus wouldn't budge. I thought, "What next?"

It wasn't long in coming. From an elevated railroad trestle, throwing distance away, came a barrage of heavy stones, called ballast. The attack was well planned, except for the terrible racket it made when it hit the metal bus. The trestle being above us, the noise of the falling stones aroused the neighborhood, and that was a lot of people. Our antagonists—other boys from the same project—having made their point, suddenly disappeared leaving us with shattered glass and plenty of fear. A couple of men came over and cleared the wheels; another removed the coat hanger from the door. We were able to drive away.

What about rock-throwers? It may be that any intrusion by outsiders on project life was thought to be a threat. So much of the outsider presence was to dupe people. Consider food stamps for example: an outsider could offer the head of a household cash at a 50% discount, and that money could be used for clothes, or liquor, or whatever she might want to buy. Things would be fine until the middle of the month when there would be no stamps left for food. The police who could have run the rascals out were themselves considered outsiders and not to be trusted or counted on. So the bus that came to take some of the boys out of the project must have also been considered a threat, and their answer was the rock attack.

Later, while we walked around the zoo, some of the boys began talking to each other loud enough for me to hear. While they hadn't known what the attackers were planning, they had known that something was going to happen. A *happening* in the project is most often serious. These boys chose to come on the trip even though they knew of the danger. They wanted me to know their club was important to them.

AN AVAILABLE GUN

Winnie called. This time it was from the Audy Home, a large austere building on the southwest side of Chicago, a temporary holding place for juveniles in trouble. It was a sad place to visit, with overtones of unresolved violence. The young people held there would be waiting with members of their family and a public defender, or alone with a public defender.

One of our Club members was in trouble—considerable trouble. He had held a gun directed at a woman, and demanded that she undress. His father owned the gun and had given it to his mother for her protection, since fathers couldn't live with their families in the project. It was for safety against what, at times, was rampant terror in the project. Residents believed the police were hesitant to respond to violence at the Robert Taylor Homes as they were often seen as less than the protectors the City proclaimed them to be, and to some they were just another enemy. That was the way it was then. It might even be so today.

The woman confronted by the gun was Monday Lou, the best friend of Thilda, the mother of the boy wielding the gun. Monday Lou was a frequent visitor to Thilda's apartment and knew the family well. Therefore, it was perfectly natural that she would open her door to the young man and invite him into her home. The young man with the gun was named Franklin, and he was twelve years old. He didn't know why he did it. When Monday Lou saw the gun pointed at her, she was terrified. Then, as she began to undress, she gained some composure and was able to talk to Franklin. She told him how much she liked his mother and father and what a beautiful family they were. She told him how fine a young man she thought he was. She told him she would continue to undress if he would just put the gun on the table next to him so she wouldn't start crying. She said she didn't want to start crying and screaming because people might hear. The message got through. Franklin abandoned his idea, fled the apartment, returned home, and put the gun back in its hiding place. He waited, not knowing what to expect.

Monday Lou, badly frightened, reported the incident to the police and that's how we all wound up at the Audy Home waiting to appear before a judge. The two women, Thilda and Monday Lou, were sympathetic to each other. They called and asked Winnie, their social worker friend, what they should say and what they should do. Winnie didn't know how to advise them, so she called me. Hearing the facts, I didn't know what to do either. We did decide, however, that we would appear together rather than be represented by an appointed legal counsel. We were strengthened in this resolve by force of numbers. We hoped the judge would realize that we were all *family*. Monday Lou was most generous in appearing with us. She had still not recovered fully from looking into a gun barrel pointed at her.

It turned out that the judge we eventually stood before was someone I knew, a highly respected jurist, and in the most difficult of venues. Seeing me in such strange surroundings, he called me up to the bench.

"What are you doing here?" he asked.

I explained as best I could—first regarding the problem, and then of my involvement with the Club member defendant.

"What do you think?" the judge asked.

I had nothing to say or suggest about the problem before us, so I said, "I think caring about people and trying to carry out your legal responsibility must be difficult, and at times even heartbreaking."

He replied that sometimes it was, but that in this particular case, it was apple-pie easy. He asked me to step down, and we all stood before him.

First, the judge spoke to young Franklin. He told him to raise his eyes, and look at the judge, and keep them there. He told him to listen closely to every word that was said. He then spoke to the mother and Monday Lou. He asked for their help. He wanted to know how they felt about the situation and what they thought should be done. With his encouragement, they spoke their minds. The boy was mixed up—he needed to have a better understanding of himself and the danger of his misdeed. The gun, they said, should be returned to Franklin's father. The friend, Monday Lou, should receive an apology from the boy, and finally, both mother and friend said they would keep a sharp lookout to see that Franklin kept out of trouble.

The judge thanked Monday Lou and Thilda for their help and gave them their instructions. Thilda was to return home, unload the gun and look for its registered number.

"Understand," the judge said, "Don't call this court and tell us the gun is missing, or lost, or stolen."

The judge then ordered Thilda to phone the bailiff and give him the registered number. "I mean today," he said.

If the gun turned out to be unregistered, the bailiff would have Thilda deliver the gun to the court and a warrant would be issued for her husband's arrest. If the gun turned out to be registered to her husband, the bailiff would give her further instructions. She was instructed to keep the empty gun until the bailiff called to tell her that she could return it to her husband. The bailiff would then phone the husband to inform him of the jeopardy he had placed himself and his family in by allowing them to have possession of his gun, and that he could go to jail. If, as the owner of the gun, the husband understood and admitted that he made a mistake, he would be told to retrieve the gun and keep it to himself. If he gave the bailiff any "lip," the bailiff would direct

Thilda to return the gun to the court where it would be kept in the custody of the judge until such time as he saw fit to release it.

In addition, the judge ruled that Franklin would be placed on probation until further notice. His mother was to know where he was at all times. All of us were ordered back to court in three weeks. The judge set the date and time. He then said that Winnie and I could report by phone, and that Monday Lou had a choice—she could phone or appear in court. The mother and son were instructed to come before him in person on the appointed date. The case was dismissed until then. Winnie took the others back to the project.

Three weeks later, the gun proved to be registered to Franklin's father who, having apologized for his mistake in giving it to his wife, was allowed to recover his gun. Monday Lou phoned the court and said she was satisfied with the way things were working out. Winnie and I made perfunctory calls to the court. Mother and son were released with emphasis on the boy's behavior. For the judge, our case was a piece of cake.

Each day, our newspapers and television record the human tragedies of people who seek justice from the Audy Home Family Court. It's a place that breaks your heart.

As for Franklin, the young man grew up, joined the police academy, is now a sergeant in the Chicago police force—and carries a gun.

HARD TO CHOOSE

It was the early 1960s. The choice was to attend or not. There was to be a rally for Dr. Martin Luther King, Jr., held between the high-rises at the Robert Taylor Homes. It wasn't going to be an easy choice for the young men of the Club, since their mothers would be involved.

It sort of went like this: the family sustenance came from government, and the government's representative was the case-worker who had the say on food stamps, monthly government assistance checks, and whether expenditures made on food and other household needs had been appropriate. The social worker also monitored conduct. But it wasn't like "Big Daddy" was on the spot, because each social worker was responsible for over 40 families.

The crux of the problem of attending the Martin Luther King, Jr. rally was *power*. A large turnout for Reverend King meant that the black society, which made up the project, was solidly behind him. The project had 26,000 people in it. On the other side stood government, and government was personified by a man who could scare you with his scowls—Chicago's longtime famous and infamous Mayor Richard J. Daley. He held the purse strings, and he didn't agree with the tactics or demands of Reverend King. That was the problem.

Now the boys and their mothers were in a pickle. The Club and its leaders believed Reverend King was a good force and had, at their last meeting, encouraged Club members to attend the rally. Most of their mothers thought otherwise. They were church-going Baptists and they were proud of Dr. King, but what about food and clothing, and what about being cut off from the source? It could happen if you stood up or challenged the status quo. Everyone knew of someone who had been taken off welfare for non-conformity. The rally for Dr. King was to be on Wednesday, and I might say those good mothers were fully aware of their problem. They loved the Club their sons belonged to; they had heard all sorts of good things about it, and were pleased that their sons were a part of it. They wondered how Mr. Club Leader would feel if their sons didn't attend the rally.

So Club members had all these factors to consider in making their decision. They had every right to say, "Life ain't easy." So they did what grownups often do, they tried to find out what the other Club members were going to do. There's power in numbers, so for safety's sake, they would go with the majority. So much for principle.

On a hot Wednesday afternoon, I went to the always crowded housing project area to attend the rally. There was a crowd assembled and most of them were in uniform—Chicago policemen. There were lots of policemen, but not too many people attending. I don't remember seeing any social workers around. Reverend King was his upbeat self, he was gracious, warm, and close to his people. Oh yes, four of the boys from the Club showed up. We stood together.

The following Saturday morning, the Club came to order about 9:15. There were 29 in attendance, an average number. They seemed subdued. Their reaction to the rally business ran the gamut. Some had stayed home and defended their mothers' positions; others were critical of their mothers who, they complained, took their problems to the Baptist minister and did whatever he said, and finally, a couple of the boys indicated that their mothers had little good to say about Reverend King. This all came from the boys; it was non-stop talk for almost two hours.

My counterpart, Winnie Freeman, the social worker, summed up the contradictory positions, put them in their proper prospective, and we all came off looking good. The Club members were relieved to turn the meeting into a discussion about where they would go next in their discovery of our great city.

It was time to go and pick up the hamburgers, fries, and soft drinks for lunch. Winnie had someplace to go in the afternoon, so we all took it easy, had our lunch, played some games down in the basement until 2 p.m. and then called it a day. Each boy received the usual carfare to take him home, and carfare for his return trip the following Saturday.

The day after our Club meeting, Winnie called to tell me she thought we all had learned about how to deal with diverse opinions during the lively discussion of Dr. King's visit. The Reverend was fighting to gain equal rights for all people. He was giving his life to attain justice for everyone, and that included the members of our Cultural Enrichment Club.

TROUBLE IN RIVER CITY

Winnie Freeman called. She was not only the social worker, but the heart of our boys' club. Winnie's call had to do with a family matter. One of the 17-year-old Club members had impregnated a young lady. This happens in the project just like it does in the suburbs.

Winnie said the social workers assigned to each of the families had come to her. Could she help in coordinating things. So Winnie agreed, and was calling to ask what evening would be suitable for me to invite the mothers of the principals out to my house. She would handle the details and all she needed was a date. We settled on Thursday evening.

Winnie arrived in her car with the grandmothers-to-be. We were introduced and sat down in the living room. My gracious and thoughtful wife had set out tea and cookies. She was busy elsewhere settling our own brood of five little rascals down for the night.

Before coming to the house, Winnie explained that I would be in for a learning experience. All I would be required to do was to say hello and listen. Listening wouldn't prove to be all that easy. "Project talk" could be a combination of English, Spanish, Haitian, or other languages—in addition to made-up words. (Project talk could differ from project to project, and location to location.)

Negotiations began. Winnie presented the problem: a baby was on its way. No one knew whether it would be a boy or a girl, and there was always the remote possibility of twins. Each of the mothers in turn addressed Winnie, and told of her current situation—how many rooms, how many living in the rooms, and what space could be made available. The two mothers had met each other at some church meeting a year before, but had not furthered their acquaintance. Winnie asked how they felt about having a new member in their family, and whether this would present a problem. Whoever took the child would add it to their dependency list, and would receive payment each month from the government. That was no light thing with them, as the payment would be less than the child would cost them. Each of these grandmothers-to-be seemed to be an open, generous person. There were some problems to be solved, however. A decision had to be made as to whose surname the child would have. Of course it would carry the name of the grandmother who would be responsible for raising the child. The grandmother who didn't take the baby was expected to provide clothes, free baby sitting, and other things during the child's first year.

There were no raised voices, but if Winnie wasn't there to guide them over the rough spots, it might have been different. There were matters to be considered like whose family was responsible for this problem, and would the girl be able to continue her classes in high school. Education was of primary importance to both grandmas. It was good to have the grandmothers there together. When only one family assumes responsibility, and the other sits idly by waiting to make problems, it's bad. It can be real bad—like both parties applying for the dependency check; or if one is a born-again Baptist, and gets to quoting the Bible as an absolute authority with no discussion of mitigating circumstances; or if either party is prone to violent acts as a solution. But there are also good grandmothers who care about family, have high moral standards, and do their best even though they are living in a most divisive neighborhood.

I listened and poured tea. They more or less forgot I was there, as they continued to talk, broadening their discussion to project matters. They could have stayed all night on that subject. When they did leave, it had been agreed. The maternal grandmother-to-be would take the child. The principals in this situation—the young lady and our Club member—would be told how matters were decided.

Time has a way of working things out. The child was a girl. Today she is a junior in college.

The Glow of Embers

.

LET'S TALK TURKEY

The more we came to know each other, the closer we became. The members of the Cultural Enrichment Club were asking if the group would be getting together for Thanksgiving. I talked it over with Winnie and she said, "Sure." We would have our own Orange Bowl/Sugar Bowl/Rose Bowl attraction with a slight difference. Instead of a New Year's Day style football fest, we would have a Cranberry Bowl. It would be a touch football game held in the park with cheeseburgers and Chicken McNuggets. Cookies and Kool-Aid would be brought from home. We planned our celebrations for Thanksgiving morning.

I bought three clothes poles and we used them to make the goal post for kicking extra points, just like the pros do. Back then, you would buy wooden poles to support the clothesline out in the backyard. Those clean clothes wafting in the breeze were a joy to see (today they're hidden in a machine to dry). We also made markers to define the playing area, painting them in the basement (a mess).

When Thanksgiving arrived, we had the park all to ourselves, and we were as ready as ready could be. We even had a fan to cheer us—Winnie—who commented, "Well, at least it isn't raining." A bit short of a roaring crowd effect!

Game morning, using the carfare they had been given at the previous Saturday's meeting, about 25 Club members arrived at my home an hour ahead of schedule. The game itself didn't seem all that important to them; it was the McNugget chicken feast that set the tone. It was Thanksgiving, and just like the rest of America, they were celebrating. For many of those young men it was a first time.

The football game was supposed to top the day's activities. In the project, games were played like "pump, pump, pull-away" or tag (which they played by hitting the other guy with a stone). With the exception of boxing, there were few black heroes in professional sports for the boys to emulate. Jackie Robinson was just opening up baseball. So our touch football game was a learning process: how to hold a football, how to throw a football, and how to catch one. They all knew how to run, it was part of life in the project. We divided into two teams. It was arranged that I would quarterback one team, and we hoped Winnie would quarterback the other. That was one time we couldn't talk Winnie into getting involved in one of our schemes. She said cheering was more important. So I threw the passes for one side, and when the ball changed hands so did I. We did a lot of improvising. The players were enthusiastic, but didn't seem to care about winning, or even about the score. Their mothers weren't aware of sports—that was a part of the white man's world—and the boys' fathers were unwelcome at the project. That's the way things were then.

A couple of years later, my sons and their friends joined Club members at the Cranberry Bowl game. The teams selected to play each other were integrated. Now a new element was added to sports—winning; and winning was paramount to everything else! A valuable lesson in life was being learned by the Club members—play or work to win. As the game's referee, I became everyone's enemy. You can't win 'em all!

After we had exhausted ourselves, we waited for Winnie to return from McDonald's with our treats. She would make the occasion as festive as she could for the boys, contributing a large box of candy on her own for desert. Winnie never missed a chance to explain and demand social graces, and she did it in a way that made the boys appreciate and accept her efforts to help them.

She would say, "Hey now, no grabbing for food," "Keep your mouth closed while you're eating," and, "Be sure to pick up any papers you drop." She sure knew how to work with those boys, and always to their betterment.

When the game was over and the food was eaten, we would sit down together. Winnie would say, "Mr. Cronin, tell us a story." Since I'm Irish, I always came prepared.

Afterwards, Winnie and I would drive the boys back to their homes in the project. This meant we would make double trips back and forth. It also meant that with both of us gone, part of the group was left on its own. Whenever this happened, Winnie would gather the boys around her. She would take time, while talking, to look each of them in the eye, and tell them what fine young men they were, how important the Club was to them, and what behavior was expected of them. If any boy tried to goof off, it was the responsibility of the rest of the group to set him straight. Love meant respect for others. The boys knew Winnie loved them.

When the Cranberry Bowl celebration was over, it was back to the project for Cultural Enrichment Club members. After we had said goodbye to the boys, I asked Winnie if she had any plans for the day. She replied, "Turkey, trimmings, and relatives."

DOG PADDLE

It was a big day for them, it was a big day for me. We were going away to a camp for a week—thirty-five Club members, Winnie, and myself. The boys and I had now been friends for some time. The idea for the trip became possible when our borrowed bus was made available to us for a week.

The Club gathered at the usual place—35th Street and State. A few of the boys had suitcases; most had their things in brown paper bags. As the leader of the group, I intended to pick up the Jesuit high school bus we had planned to borrow for the trip. However, when I arrived at the school, I discovered the bus being towed away for major repairs. All was almost lost.

At the time, I headed a small construction business. Not too small, though—we had about 20 trucks. I called our trusted superintendent, Harold, and explained the dilemma, and asked if he could commandeer a stake truck and driver from some job site and rescue me. Time was passing as I waited for his return call. When it came, he said he had found two pick-up trucks with drivers; where should he send them?

"35th and State," I said.

We would all assemble at 35th Street, including the boys (and some of their mothers who had come to check us out), and of course Mrs. Winnie Freeman, the Club's social worker. Winnie knew the boys, and the boys knew her, and loved her. The two pick-ups with drivers in work clothes were there; and we commandeered Winnie's black Chevy, asking her to drive it to the camp in order to accommodate all of the boys. My own car was a big black Cadillac, the kind mostly owned by rich people, many of whom were gangsters. (I wasn't that rich and I wasn't a gangster, but it was fun sometimes having people think so.) So we set off—myself in the lead, two pick-ups, and Winnie at the rear. The Holy Family Camp was 90 miles away. All went well, and we arrived at our destination.

Before arriving, we passed through the sister cities of St. Joe and Benton Harbour. Little did we know! When we got to the Camp, we drove in and before we were unloaded, all hell broke lose. Police cars with their sirens were setting up a racket and were coming from every direction. They weren't fooling either. Someone had called to tell them where we were and here they came, in force. Some policemen got out of their patrol cars with their night sticks in hand. The leader centered on me and asked what I thought I was doing. You see, in Benton Harbour, there had been a race riot the night before, including a killing. Feelings couldn't have been more tense. We were thought to be invaders from Chicago coming to slug it out against the white community. No one who saw us go through town took time to see how old the boys were. It was enough that they were black.

One close-up look at the boys and me calmed the state troopers' fears. They asked us what was up and when we told why we were there, they said we were certainly welcome to stay and for our own protection they would station two State Police cars at the entrance overnight. The way rumors grow, a counterattack might be brewing at the moment in some local bar. The evening newspaper gave us some nice publicity, and we settled down for our week together.

The camp was located on property bordering Lake Michigan that had been bequeathed to the Catholic Archdiocese. The cardinal then gave the property to the Knights of Peter Claver to use—this was a black organization made up of Catholics. Its counterpart in the white community was the well-known Knights of Columbus. The Knights of Columbus blackballed Negroes from membership, including the all-American captain of Notre Dame's basketball team. He was a great student, a great everything—but he was black. That's the way it was thirty years ago. Things have changed since then. The Peter Claver Knights offered us the use of this camp which they had been given. There were about 15 small cabins; and a new long metal building with a kitchen, a large eating area, and a large shower and bathroom—enough shower and bathroom facilities for the Camp people.

The next morning, to my surprise, my son Christopher showed up. Chris was working as a roofer in the family business to help pay for his college education. Knowing his father, he had told Harold, the superintendent, that he could do more for the roofing company by being at the Camp and keeping an eye on *that kook*, his father. He arrived in the nick of time. Someone reported that the boys had gone down the side of the dune to the shores of Lake Michigan. Chris asked me if the boys knew how to swim. He didn't wait for an answer; he was down the dune in a flash. Later that morning, after saying goodbye to our state troopers and assuring them that I would call them rather than do something foolish, I finished some chores, and walked to the top of the dune. There was only one boy in the water and Chris was teaching him to swim—only 34 more to go.

Winnie was in charge of food, bedding, and I don't know what else—everything. My dear black friend wanted me to take her shopping to get food, lots of it. We went to a local supermarket. She gave the orders, I carried them out—two dozen loaves of bread, lots of hot dogs, beans, macaroni, milk, Kool-Aid—for a start. While I was bringing food back to our carts, I noticed I had drawn the attention of four women shoppers. I realized they were staring and were not smiling. So when Winnie came back to the carts laden with food, I told her that although she didn't know it, and I didn't know it, we apparently were married—or worse! At least that was the impression I was getting from those dour-looking women who weren't moving, just standing there. (Of course, I was complimented since Winnie was at least fifteen or twenty years younger, and she was pretty.) I didn't ask her what she thought of the arrangement.

Anyway, to disperse our forbidding group I turned to them with a full smile and said in as loud a voice as I could, while walking towards them, "Helen, how good to see you—it's been so long." Before I got to where the group was standing, they had scurried away in every direction. If there was a Helen among them, she would, let's say, have been a bit uncomfortable.

Dinner at the camp with Winnie was something. A bell was rung and we all had five minutes to wash and be seated. Winnie sat at one end of the table. I sat at the other, and Chris sat somewhere on the side. Winnie and her five selected servers were in the kitchen. The servers would bring out our paper plates of food. I was served first, then the official host for the dinner who was seated next to me, and the rest in an orderly fashion.

We all waited until Winnie joined us. She nodded to one of the boys and he said grace. We all said, "Amen," and dove into the food. Mine had been served first—it was the coldest.

I had been raised in a good family where my mother would say, "Eat your food before it gets cold." Well, if you're hungry enough, you'll eat it hot or cold.

Winnie knew boys. There was a second helping for those who wanted it—the selected servers handled this operation. The designated host who was sitting next to me was in charge of dinner conversation. He began by listing about five subjects to be discussed. They ranged from war and baseball players to whatever they found wrong with their mothers. To talk on the subject, we would raise the hand we weren't eating with, and wait to be recognized by the host. After naming the subjects, the host did not participate in the discussion, he just pointed out who got to speak next. When my hand went up, it wasn't all that important; the host wanted to get in good with his own buddies. When

Winnie had filled us up—dessert and all—we sat there and waited impatiently.

Finally she said, "Well, Mr. Cronin, should we let these devils go?" Rules were over, and we ran pell-mell to the baseball diamond.

I was the umpire, and nobody, but nobody, liked me. When I said, "safe," those on one side of the decision smiled, but the losers shouted and booed. Even Chris, out there playing right field, joined in the booing. It was a no-win situation for me. After the game, we all put on our swimming trunks, or clean underwear, and went swimming or wading in Lake Michigan. A lot of the boys could do the dog paddle. When Chris was teaching them how to swim and found an adept pupil, that boy immediately became a teacher of the dog paddle to another boy. Those who never learned how to swim drank a lot of water before we gave up on them.

In the evening there was basketball on an outdoor court, and also a court of a different kind where Winnie reigned. She knew how the homesick boys felt and what to do. She could usually get her arms around them all. (Winnie had been married a couple of years before I met her. She didn't think she could have children. With the boys in the Club she had a bigger family, as it turned out, than she had expected.)

One morning later in the week, Winnie asked me to go along on her inspection tour of the small motel accommodations where the boys were staying. By small, I mean they had no plumbing facilities. They used a common john in the metal building. As management people, Winnie and I each had our own cabin—with plumbing. These were the former owner's private quarters. Thank God! During our inspection, I noticed they were a lot more orderly than I (or their mothers back home) might expect. "Master Sergeant Lady Winnie" was not lenient. I was there to reinforce her warning that I would be paying a visit. I couldn't imagine any of the boys being frightened of me. When I tried to think of any of the boys I could possibly scare, one came to mind—little roly-poly Johnnie. You know, it's thirty years later and all these years he's been calling faithfully to tell his "Pop" how he's doing.

Good times go quickly. On the last night, Winnie found reasons to give each boy a prize, something he could wear, like a shirt, or socks, or scarf. In the morning, it was back to the city and life in the project, and for the boys to tell their mothers about their vacations. Winnie and I went our separate ways. We both took the day off.

Winnifred Freeman
1933–1968

After three and a half years together, Winnie, who was indeed the very heart of the Club, became sick and quickly died. Some friends provided station wagons and the whole Club was able to go to the wake. It was held in Winnie's neighborhood at a nice funeral parlor mortuary. It was also my neighborhood. When we arrived, the undertaker had made arrangements. Winnie's friends must have told him about the Club, and that we would probably show up. There was a large crowd inside and out. We were led up front where a space had been made for us. When the line of the bereaved shortened, we were invited to join in viewing the body. Winnie seemed to be telling me to stand next to the casket in case any of the boys needed help. It wasn't a funeral service we were attending, it was just the wake. The undertaker, however, asked me to say a few words.

I spoke to the boys, but loud enough for all to hear. It wasn't much, just about a phrase Winnie had used that we all knew well. When she was ending a sentence, she would say, "y' hear now?" So I told the boys to remember Winnie and "y' hear now?" and if trouble came into their lives, to think of what she would say and then say to themselves, "y' hear now?"

A lovely social worker, Ruth, was assigned to take Winnie's place and work with the boys. Unfortunately, by a strange coincidence, she died of cancer in a year. The assignment seemed to lose its appeal to social workers. We had been meeting on Wednesday afternoons at the project, and Saturday mornings at my home for four years. We all had suffered the loss of Winnie and Ruth. My own enthusiasm waned, and the Club dissolved over the next six months.

A Change for the Better

During the era of the Club, the community, the city of Chicago, and even the country, were caught up in change. It was the time of civil rights. Even though all of us involved in the Cultural Enrichment Club tried to make our presence in the neighborhood as inconspicuous as possible, it didn't work. The young men would get off the bus at different streets, and walk to the house in ones and twos. They would leave the same way. Like everything else, we made a game of it. Those walking the furthest distance to get on a bus would leave first, followed by the ones who caught their buses at streets closer to my house. The bus that took the boys back to the project would make regular stops along the route, so if we timed it right, the separate groups would be picked up block after block, and they would all end up on the same bus.

Then it happened. One evening when my wife Mary and I were attending a high school play, a friend came to us and said, "They're burning a cross at your front door."

We hurried home. It turned out to be a crude attempt. The pieces of the cross were made of hardwood. The vandals probably had a tough time nailing through it. They would have even less of a chance of getting it to burn. They had apparently poured gasoline on it and set it afire. When the fluid had burned up, the fiery cross went out. The flames must have lasted less than a minute. It was frightening for Mary, particularly since our children were small and our little daughter did a lot of crying. There was no damage.

During the night, I stayed by the phone to answer the crazy's phone calls. A week later, shortly after Mary and I had left for a party, they did a better job of it. There was a big tree on our front lawn with a trunk that went up about eighteen feet before branches and leaves appeared. The tree trunk had been sprayed with gasoline as far up as possible and then set ablaze. It stopped traffic until it burned out. The tree wasn't damaged, but we didn't even get to stay at the party long enough for a drink.

Again, there were phone calls through the night. Those hoodlums were interfering with my private life. They were young men who had decided to do something other than talk like their parents did, and teenagers are prone to pranks.

A black family had recently moved into our neighborhood, and their young son dropped by at our house to see if he could join the Club. The members voted, and he was accepted. Our new Club member brought a problem with him, though. It had to do with the acceptance of black students at our parish grammar school. Blacks were new to the area and panic was just around the corner. One sub-zero morning, Mary and I, along with several black mothers, made a call at the school. We found things cold inside as well as out. The school principal, a nun, and a fine person, was sympathetic, but her vow of obedience forbade her from acting against the pastor's orders, and the pastor was vacationing in Florida.

Undaunted, and now led by a professional, the Director of the Catholic Interracial Council, we all went downtown to the office of the Catholic Board of Education. The cardinal's representative listened to our plea which was to allow black Catholic children to attend the parish school if their families were residents of the parish. We were told that our pastor's position was one of gradualism. Kindergarten children would be accepted in the present year, and first graders the following year. The children of the black mothers in our entourage that day were of all ages.

Again, we got the "sorry" treatment. It was still sub-zero and since we had no place else to go and there was nothing more we could do, we all went home.

About six o'clock that evening, I received a telephone call from the sister who was principal of the grammar school. She told me that all the black children who lived in the parish could be brought to school in the morning, and they would be enrolled. Hallelujah! Since I could feel that she was happy to call me, I asked what caused the change. She said that the pastor had called from Florida, and issued the order. What I found out later was that our good luck had to do with politics and our new president, Jack Kennedy. The church was hoping that a voucher system for private education might be set in motion. Small as our effort was, local church authorities decided if we took our case to the news-papers or radio, it might have a negative effect on the voucher effort.

When I said "hallelujah" before, it was premature. I called the black parents with the good news, but their reception was mixed. They wanted a meeting that night. It was still sub-zero outside so I was glad to host the get-together. When they arrived, they made their concern clear. The victory was all well and good, but it would be their children who would be going into what could be hostile territory. (If this long sub-zero day isn't wearing you out, you're a better man than I am.)

It was nine o'clock—we had won the battle, but we were losing the war. I called a friend. (God bless friends.) He was one of Chicago's highest ranking police officers—I think he was a commissioner. He listened to what I had to way. He was black and he was Catholic. (This is the truth.)

He said he'd be right over if his car would start, "Just don't let those parents go home."

He arrived a little while later. He could talk to them about where he and they had come from. Mary and I went into the kitchen to make some tea for our guests. He assured them that police and police cars would be on hand at the school the next day, and that he would make an appearance himself when school let out. He saved the day.

Next morning, the children—eleven of them—were enrolled. The following day, the pastor made a surprise return to his winter parish and parishioners. He visited his school and went to each classroom. He told the children of their responsibility to God, to their teachers and to him, and how to welcome the new students. Everyone in the school was to love one another—well, at least no hitting!

It gradually worked out. Washington never passed voucher legislation, but the try was a godsend to our little group. The parish grammar school had an enrollment of close to six hundred at that time. It's a little less today, still an integrated school—with only about eleven whites in attendance.

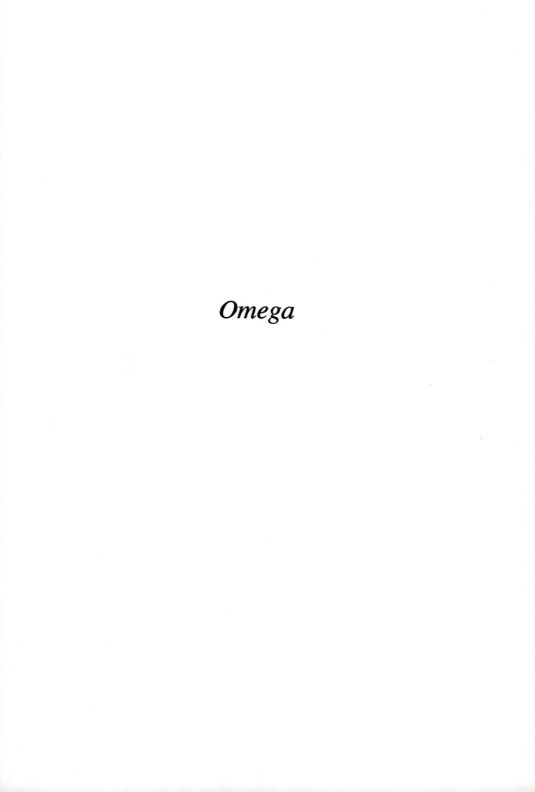

Omega

The Glow of Embers

THE NIGHT IS MINE TO GREET THE DAWN

What a joy!
The whole night is mine.
All these years I've considered it a treasure;
To be awake and to be happy,
And now—

This night, tomorrow, and
All the remaining tomorrows are precious;
I live for them, I wait for them,
I grasp them—
For at night I write!

The Glow of Embers

SHARE

The Glow of Embers

WITH FRIENDS

Available at the Following Locations
Credit Card Orders Accepted

Brent Books
309 W. Washington St.
Chicago, IL 60606
Adam Brent, Mgr.
(312) 364-0126
list price delivery to gold coast area

MacIntosh Book Shop
2365 Periwinkle Way
Sanibel Island, FL 33957
Phillip Armitage, Mgr.
(941) 472-1447

Lincoln Park Books
2423 N. Clark St.
Chicago, IL 60614
Joel Jacobson, Mgr.
(312) 477-7087

U.S. Catholic Book Store
160 N. Wabash
Chicago, IL 60601
Jim Kirkpatrick, Mgr.
(312) 855-1908

List Price
– $9.85 –

Additional Charge for Postage and Handling
(enclosure card included)
– $3.50 –

Island Graphics
Printing & Design
459 Periwinkle Way
Sanibel Island, Florida 33957